• HISTORY OF AFRICA •

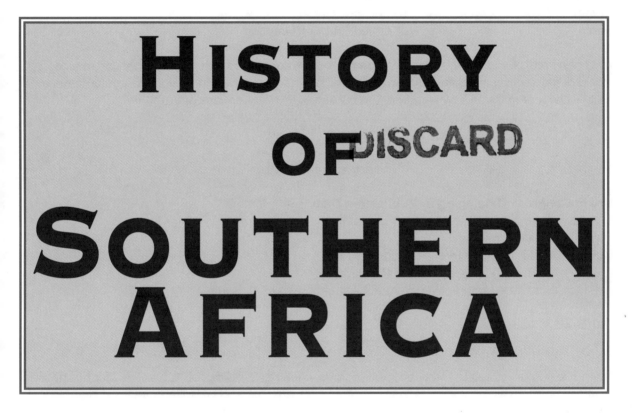

HISTORY OF DISCARD

SOUTHERN AFRICA

THE DIAGRAM GROUP

Facts On File, Inc.

History of Africa: History of Southern Africa
Copyright © 2003 by The Diagram Group

Diagram Visual Information Ltd

Editorial director:	Denis Kennedy
Editor:	Peter Harrison
Contributor:	Ann Kramer
Consultant:	Keith Lye
Indexer:	Martin Hargreaves
Senior designer:	Lee Lawrence
Designers:	Claire Bojczuk, Gill Shaw
Illustrators:	Kathy McDougall, Graham Rosewarne
Research:	Neil McKenna, Patricia Robertson

Facts On File, Inc.
132 West 31st Street
New York NY 10001

Library of Congress Cataloging-in-Publication Data
History of Southern Africa / The Diagram Group.
    p. cm. – (History of Africa)
  Includes bibliographical references and index.
  ISBN 0-8160-5060-0 (set) – ISBN 0-8160-5065-1
  1. Africa, Southern–History–Miscellanea. I. Diagram Group. II. Series.

DT1075 .H57 2003

2002035209

Facts On File books are available at special discounts when purchased in bulk quantities for businesses, associations, institutions, or sales promotions. Please call our Special Sales Department in New York at 212/967-8800 or 800/322-8755.

You can find Facts On File on the World Wide Web at: http://www.factsonfile.com

Printed in the United States of America

EB DIAG 10 9 8 7 6 5 4 3 2 1

Contents

FOREWORD

The six-volume History of Africa series has been designed as a companion set to the Peoples of Africa series. Although, of necessity, there is some overlap between the two series, there is also a significant shift in focus. Whereas Peoples of Africa focuses on ethnographic issues, that is the individual human societies which make up the continent, History of Africa graphically presents a historical overview of the political forces that shaped the vast continent today.

History of Southern Africa starts off with a description of the region in depth, including its religions, land, climate, and the languages spoken there today, with particular relevance to the colonial legacy as it affected the spoken word region-by-region. There then follows an overview of events from prehistory to the present day, and a brief discussion of the various historical sources that help us to learn about the past.

The major part of the book comprises an in-depth examination of the history of the region from the first humans through the early civilizations or chiefdoms; the development of trade with other countries; the arrival of European colonists, and the effect this had on the indigenous peoples; the struggles for independence in the last century; and the current political situation in the nation, or island, states in the 21st century.

Interspersed throughout the main text of the book are special features on a variety of political topics or historical themes which bring the region to life, such as the Iron-Age settlement of Mapungubwe, the civilization of Great Zimbabwe, the Great Trek, Zulu warriors, and Zimbabwe today.

Throughout the book the reader will also find timelines which list major events combined with maps, diagrams and illustrations, presented in two color form throughout, which help to explain these events in more detail, and place them within the context of world events. Finally, there is a glossary which defines unfamiliar words used in the book, and a comprehensive index. Taken together with the other five volumes in this series, *History of Southern Africa* will provide the reader with a memorable snapshot of Africa as a continent with a rich history.

Dates

In this book, we use the dating system BCE – Before Common Era – and CE – Common Era. 1 CE is the same year as 1 AD. We have used this system because many people in Southern Africa do not recognize the Christian dating system BC – Before Christ – and AD – *Anno Domini* – because they are members of other faiths.

A key issue

Apartheid ("apartness"), the policy, which kept black and white South Africans separate, had profound political, social, and cultural effects on South Africa and its people. Owing to its importance, one whole chapter in this volume is devoted to the subject of apartheid. The chapter describes the introduction of apartheid, its implementation in South Africa from 1948 until it was repealed in 1991, and its effect on other countries in the region.

Graffiti
From 1948–1991, many South Africans chose not to vote in protest against the apartheid regime under which they lived.

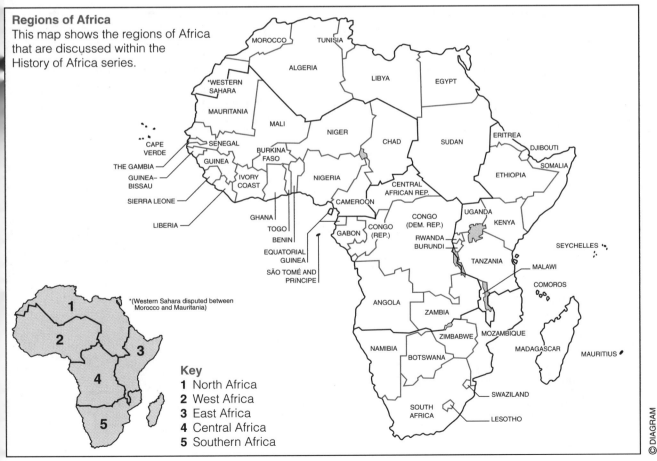

Regions of Africa
This map shows the regions of Africa that are discussed within the History of Africa series.

*(Western Sahara disputed between Morocco and Mauritania)

Key
1 North Africa
2 West Africa
3 East Africa
4 Central Africa
5 Southern Africa

© DIAGRAM

Land

Southern Africa is a vast region consisting mainly of ancient volcanic rocks. Landscapes vary considerably from the dry Namib and Kalahari Deserts in the west and center, through to the high Drakensberg Mountains in the east, the fertile grasslands of the interior, and the swamps and sandy beaches of Mozambique. Most people in Southern Africa live either on the coastal strips or the inland plateaus.

The Atlantic Ocean borders Southern Africa to the west, and the Indian Ocean to the south and east. Most of the interior of the country consists of rolling plateaus (uplands), including the Southern Plateau, which covers most of South Africa, Namibia, Botswana, and Zimbabwe. In South Africa, the Southern Plateau divides into four regions: the Highveld, Middleveld, Lowveld, and the Transvaal Basin. The height of the Plateau varies from about 3,000 ft (1,000 m) above sea level to a maximum of about 6,000 ft (1,800 m).

Running along the edge of the Southern Plateau is a mountainous area called the Great Escarpment. In Lesotho and eastern South Africa the Escarpment forms the Drakensberg Mountains, which contain the highest mountains in the region. The Cape Mountains are in southwest South Africa and contain Table Mountain, which overlooks Cape Town.

There are many rivers in the region, including the Zambezi, Limpopo, Orange, and Vaal. All the rivers run into the sea except the Okavango River, which runs inland into a desert.

South Africa's coastline is generally rocky, formed where the mountains drop down to the sea. There are natural harbors at Table Bay, Algoa Bay, and Maputo Bay. By contrast, Mozambique has a low shoreline of sandy beaches, swamps and lagoons. On Namibia's coastline, desert and sea meet to create huge sand dunes.

Madagascar, the world's fourth largest island, lies 250 miles (400 km) to the east of Southern Africa. The island contains a central highland and a broad coastal plain in the west.

Southern Plateau

- Plateau land below 4,500 ft (1,400 m)
- Plateau land above 4,500 ft (1,400 m)

Highlands

- Highland rim over 4,500 ft (1,400 m)
- Highland rim between 1,200 and 4,500 ft (350–1,400 m)

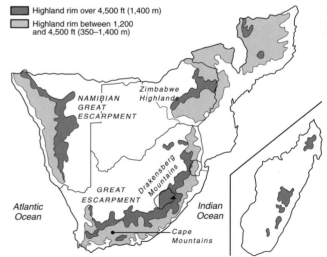

Climate

Climate in Southern Africa is as varied as the landscape and each region has its own particular conditions, ranging from the tropical, warm, wet climate of eastern Madagascar through to the desert climate of parts of Namibia and South Africa.

Average temperatures range from about 13 °C (55 °F) in Cape Town during July through to more than 38 °C (100 °F) in Botswana in summer. Snow falls on the high peaks of South Africa and Lesotho during winter. Most of Southern Africa has rain during the summer, with most falling near the Indian Ocean. Inland, most regions have less than 30 in (76 cm) of rain each year.

But there are extremes. Every year some 126 in (325 cm) of rain falls in Antananarivo, capital of Madagascar; by contrast the Namib Desert has less than 1 in (2.5 cm) annually.

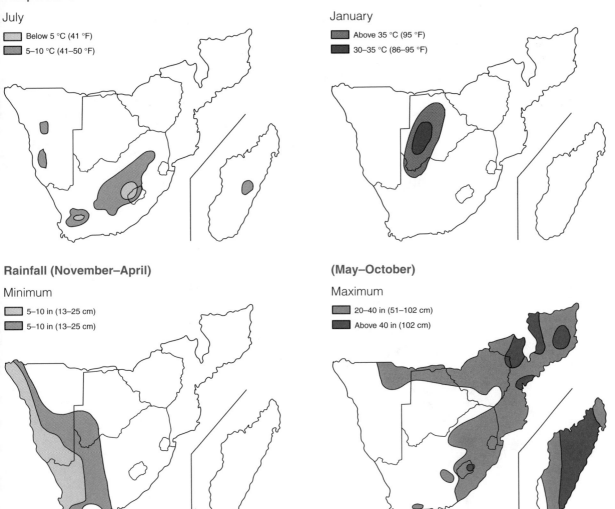

Temperature

July
- Below 5 °C (41 °F)
- 5–10 °C (41–50 °F)

January
- Above 35 °C (95 °F)
- 30–35 °C (86–95 °F)

Rainfall (November–April)

Minimum
- 5–10 in (13–25 cm)
- 5–10 in (13–25 cm)

(May–October)

Maximum
- 20–40 in (51–102 cm)
- Above 40 in (102 cm)

© DIAGRAM

7

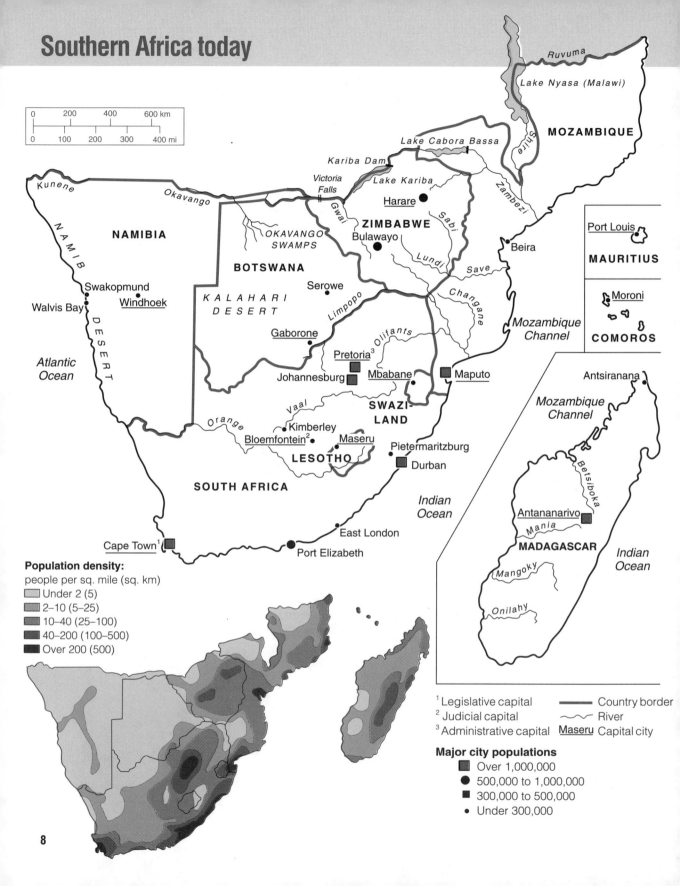

Scale:
0 — 200 — 400 — 600 km
0 — 100 — 200 — 300 — 400 mi

Kunene

Okavango

NAMIBIA

N A M I B   D E S E R T

Swakopmund

Walvis Bay

Windhoek

Atlantic Ocean

OKAVANGO SWAMPS

BOTSWANA

K A L A H A R I   D E S E R T

Serowe

Gaborone

Victoria Falls

Gwai

Kariba Dam

Lake Kariba

ZIMBABWE

Harare

Bulawayo

Sabi

Lundi

Save

Changane

Limpopo

Olifants

Pretoria[3]

Johannesburg

Mbabane

Maputo

SWAZI-LAND

Vaal

Kimberley

Bloemfontein[2]

Maseru

LESOTHO

Orange

SOUTH AFRICA

Pietermaritzburg

Durban

Indian Ocean

East London

Cape Town[1]

Port Elizabeth

Ruvuma

Lake Nyasa (Malawi)

Shire

MOZAMBIQUE

Lake Cabora Bassa

Zambezi

Beira

Mozambique Channel

Port Louis

MAURITIUS

Moroni

COMOROS

Mozambique Channel

Antsiranana

Betsiboka

Antananarivo

Mania

MADAGASCAR

Mangoky

Onilahy

Indian Ocean

Population density:
people per sq. mile (sq. km)
- Under 2 (5)
- 2–10 (5–25)
- 10–40 (25–100)
- 40–200 (100–500)
- Over 200 (500)

[1] Legislative capital
[2] Judicial capital
[3] Administrative capital

Country border
River
Maseru Capital city

Major city populations
- Over 1,000,000
- 500,000 to 1,000,000
- 300,000 to 500,000
- Under 300,000

Botswana

Botswana is a landlocked country in the center of Southern Africa. Most people are Tswana, or Batswana. Other ethnic groups include Khoisan or Khung, and Shona peoples. It gained independence from Britain in 1966 as the Republic of Botswana.

Comoros

Consisting of four main islands, Comoros lies in the Indian Ocean off the coast of Mozambique. In 1975, three islands – Grand Comore, Anjouan, and Mohéli – declared independence from France. The fourth island, Mayotte, remained a dependency.

Lesotho

A landlocked mountainous country, Lesotho is entirely surrounded by South Africa. In 1966 Lesotho (called Basutoland under colonial rule) gained independence from Britain, as the Kingdom of Lesotho. The country is a constitutional monarchy.

Madagascar

The island nation of Madagascar became independent from France in 1960, as the Malagasy Republic. In 1972 the army seized power and in 1975 the country was renamed the Republic of Madagascar, under President Didier Ratsiraka.

Mauritius

Initially colonized by the Dutch and French, in 1810 Mauritius became a British colony. In 1968 it became independent, and in 1992 it became a republic, largely due to the efforts of Anerood Jugnauth and his Militant Socialist Movement (MSM) party.

Mozambique

In 1975 Mozambique achieved independence from Portugal after many years of armed struggle led by the Front for the Liberation of Mozambique (FRELIMO). Following independence FRELIMO governed the country as a one-party Marxist state.

Namibia

Colonized by Germany in 1885, and named South West Africa, Namibia came under South African control in 1920. The country (renamed Namibia in 1968), did not finally achieve independence until 1990, the last African colony to do so.

South Africa

Formed in 1910, the Union of South Africa became an independent republic in 1961.The first democratic multiracial elections were held in 1994, when Nelson Mandela became president. Thabo Mbeki succeeded him in 1999.

Swaziland

In 1968 Swaziland achieved independence from Britain as a constitutional monarchy. In 1973 the reigning monarch Sobhuza II suspended the constitution and became absolute ruler. His successor was Mswati III, who has ruled the country since 1986.

Zimbabwe

Zimbabwe, under white minority rule from the 1920s, was declared independent in 1964. In 1980 the country became a legally independent republic, with Robert Mugabe as the first black prime minister and, later, president.

Seretse Khama, first prime minister of Botswana in 1965

Ahmed Abdallah, leader of Comoros, independent in 1975

Letsie III, king of Lesotho from 1900–1995 and 1996–present

President Tsiranana, first president of Madagascar in 1960

Anerood Jugnauth, prime minister of Mauritius in 1982

Samora Machel, president of Mozambique, 1975–1986

Sam Nujoma, president of Namibia since 1990

Nelson Mandela, president of South Africa 1994–1999

Sobhuza II, king of Swaziland from 1922–1982

Robert Mugabe, prime minister of Zimbabwe in 1980

©DIAGRAM

The languages of Southern Africa

Africa contains more languages than any other continent. More than 1,000 so-called home languages – languages native to the continent – are spoken, although they are difficult to classify. In Southern Africa, the two main language groups are Bantu and the small Khoisan language groups.

Within these two divisions are many different languages. Different ethnic groups also identify themselves by the languages they speak. The language of the Shona people, for instance, is also called Shona. Similarly, the Herero of Namibia speak a language called Herero. For historical reasons, some languages are widely spoken. Shona, for instance, is widespread because the Shona, who built Great Zimbabwe, were very influential.

European settlers, and others who arrived in Southern Africa, brought their own languages to the region and many of these are also widely spoken. Languages introduced into Southern Africa include English, French, Portuguese, Afrikaans, Urdu, Hindi, Gujarati, and Malagasy (the language of Madagascar). Afrikaans is widely spoken in South Africa, and in Namibia. Used by Dutch settlers, it evolved from 17th century Dutch and incorporated some African words as well as reflecting the experience of the Dutch in Africa. Arabic is spoken in a few parts of Southern Africa, notably Comoros.

The home languages of Africa are divided into four main families. Within these families are subfamilies, which are divided again into groups and then subgroups. The Bantu group of languages is a subgroup of the Niger-Kordofanian family. Most of the Southern African home languages fall into the Bantu group, reflecting the fact that Bantu-speaking people were well established throughout Southern Africa by the start of the Common Era.

Khoisan is the smallest of the African language families but is very well known because its language groups use highly distinctive "click" sounds, made with the tongue on various parts of the mouth. Many Bantu languages, such as Xhosa, have incorporated "click" sounds.

The diagram on the page opposite provides a very simplified classification of African languages.

Miriam Makeba
An accomplished jazz singer, Makeba's style features many of the "click" sounds used in some Southern African languages.

Tribal elders
In-depth knowledge of local customs and historical events were handed down by word of mouth from one generation to the next.

African languages

The people of Africa speak more than 1,000 different languages, most of them "home" languages native to the continent. The remaining languages, such as Arabic, English, or French, have all been introduced by settlers or invaders from Asia or Europe. The home languages are divided into four main families, within which are several subfamilies. These are then divided into groups and again into subgroups. Those languages spoken in South Africa are printed in *italic* in the charts below.

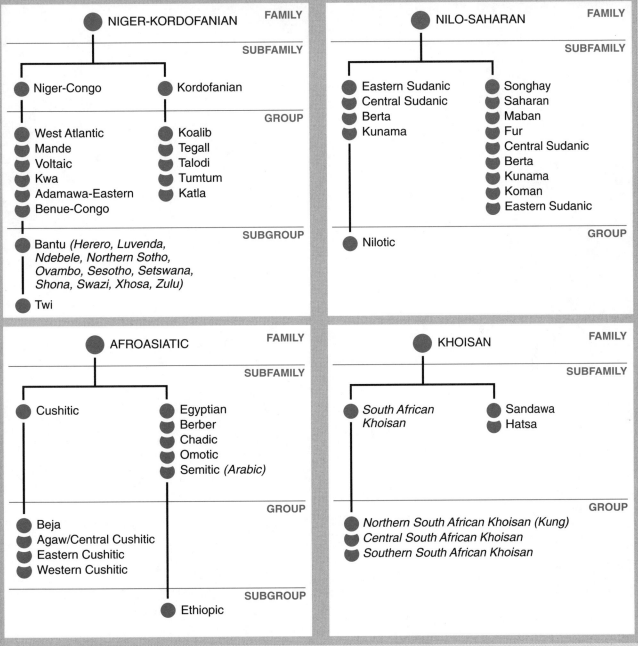

NIGER-KORDOFANIAN — FAMILY

SUBFAMILY
- Niger-Congo
- Kordofanian

GROUP
- West Atlantic
- Mande
- Voltaic
- Kwa
- Adamawa-Eastern
- Benue-Congo
- Koalib
- Tegall
- Talodi
- Tumtum
- Katla

SUBGROUP
- Bantu (*Herero, Luvenda, Ndebele, Northern Sotho, Ovambo, Sesotho, Setswana, Shona, Swazi, Xhosa, Zulu*)
- Twi

NILO-SAHARAN — FAMILY

SUBFAMILY
- Eastern Sudanic
- Central Sudanic
- Berta
- Kunama
- Songhay
- Saharan
- Maban
- Fur
- Central Sudanic
- Berta
- Kunama
- Koman
- Eastern Sudanic

GROUP
- Nilotic

AFROASIATIC — FAMILY

SUBFAMILY
- Cushitic
- Egyptian
- Berber
- Chadic
- Omotic
- Semitic (*Arabic*)

GROUP
- Beja
- Agaw/Central Cushitic
- Eastern Cushitic
- Western Cushitic

SUBGROUP
- Ethiopic

KHOISAN — FAMILY

SUBFAMILY
- *South African Khoisan*
- Sandawa
- Hatsa

GROUP
- *Northern South African Khoisan (Kung)*
- *Central South African Khoisan*
- *Southern South African Khoisan*

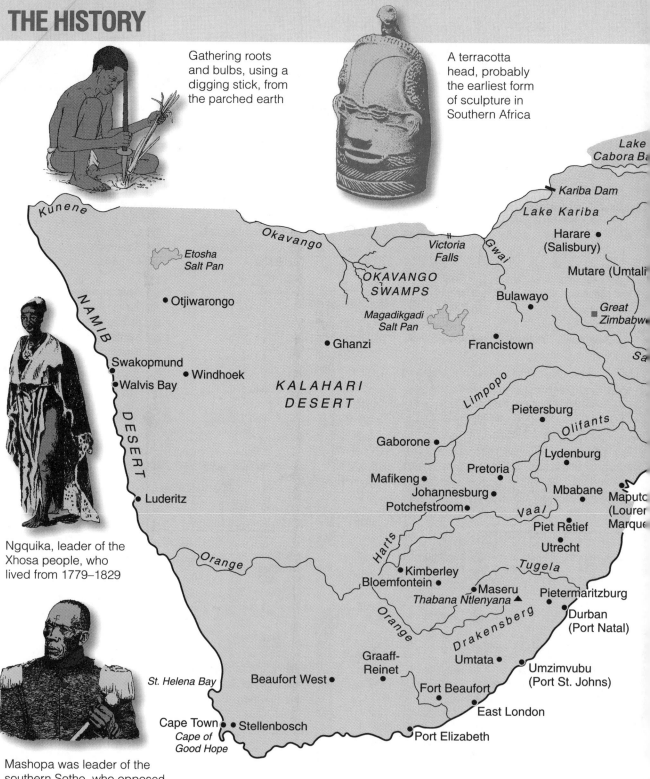

Gathering roots and bulbs, using a digging stick, from the parched earth

A terracotta head, probably the earliest form of sculpture in Southern Africa

Ngquika, leader of the Xhosa people, who lived from 1779–1829

Mashopa was leader of the southern Sotho, who opposed British rule in the Cape

Lake Cabora B...

Kariba Dam

Lake Kariba

Harare (Salisbury)

Mutare (Umtali...

Kunene

Okavango

Victoria Falls

Gwai

Bulawayo

Etosha Salt Pan

OKAVANGO SWAMPS

Great Zimbabw...

NAMIB

Otjiwarongo

Magadikgadi Salt Pan

Francistown

Sa...

Ghanzi

Swakopmund

Windhoek

KALAHARI DESERT

Limpopo

Pietersburg

Walvis Bay

Olifants

DESERT

Gaborone

Lydenburg

Pretoria

Mafikeng

Luderitz

Johannesburg

Mbabane

Maputo (Lourer... Marque...

Potchefstroom

Vaal

Piet Retief

Harts

Utrecht

Orange

Tugela

Kimberley

Bloemfontein

Maseru

Pietermaritzburg

Thabana Ntlenyana

Durban (Port Natal)

Orange

Drakensberg

Umtata

Umzimvubu (Port St. Johns)

Graaff-Reinet

St. Helena Bay

Beaufort West

Fort Beaufort

East London

Cape Town

Stellenbosch

Cape of Good Hope

Port Elizabeth

The history of Southern Africa dates back thousands of years. Archaeological sites show evidence of early hominids some four million years ago; some 36,000 years ago hunter-gatherers lived in what is now Lesotho. The earliest known inhabitants were the Khoisan but from about 200 CE, Bantu-speaking peoples arrived in the region, gradually displacing or absorbing the Khoisan. Today, most black Southern Africans are descendants of early Bantu arrivals.

European arrivals

The first Europeans did not arrive until the 16th century and when they came they found flourishing cultures. By the mid-17th century, as Dutch settlers were expanding outwards from the Cape, African nations existed in most of Southern Africa. During the 19th century, increasing numbers of British and other European colonizers arrived in the region. By the end of the 19th century, virtually the whole of Southern Africa had become European colonies.

White rule and liberation

During the colonial period, white minority rule was established in some countries, including South Africa, and what are now Namibia and Zimbabwe. During the 20th century, resistance re-emerged as black liberation movements fought to achieve independence. From the 1960s, country after country broke free from colonial rule, and by the 1990s all of what are now the ten countries of Southern Africa had achieved independence.

How we know

Information about the history of Southern Africa comes from many sources. Archaeological sites provide evidence of prehistoric peoples in the region, while rock paintings provide an insight into the lives of early hunters and farmers. Gold objects, pottery remains, and stone structures, such as those of Great Zimbabwe, give evidence of trading and other centers. Also, African elders and storytellers have always passed their history on by word of mouth from generation to generation.

Freedom fighters from FRELIMO march to victory in Mozambique

One of many children killed when policemen opened fire in the township of Soweto

©DIAGRAM

13

Events

SOUTHERN AFRICAN EVENTS	WORLD EVENTS

2 MYA–100 CE

c.1.5 mya	*Australopithecus* lives in Southern Africa	**c. 38,000 BCE** early *Homo asapiens* inhabits Europe
c.100,000 BCE	*Homo sapiens sapiens* emerges in Southern Africa	
c.34,000 BCE	Hunter-gatherers occupy what is now Lesotho	**510 BCE** Roman republic founded
c.25,000 BCE	Khoisan people produce cave paintings	
c.10,000 BCE	Advances in stone technology	**c. 30 CE** Jesus crucified

101 CE–1000 CE

200s CE	Bantu-speaking peoples arrive in southern Africa	**c. 300** Maya civilization emerges, Mexico
300s–400s CE	Bantu-speakers move into north and southeast South Africa, bringing ironworking and use of the hoe	**455** Vandals sack Rome
600s CE	Indonesians settle Madagascar	**622** Prophet Muhammad flees to Medina; Islam founded
650–1300	Iron-Age and cattle-owning "Toutswe" communities flourish in Botswana	**624** T'ang dynasty unites China
900s	Trading center Mapungubwe develops on Limpopo River	**793** Viking raids begin, Europe
1000s	Bantu-speaking people migrate to Madagascar	
1000s	Important Iron-Age settlement built in Zimbabwe	

1001–1500

1100–1300	Trading center of Mapungubwe reaches its height	**c. 1200** Inca empire, Andes
1300s–1400s	Great Zimbabwe at peak of prosperity; Muslims set up trading colonies and kingdoms in Madagascar	**1206** Genghis Khan begins Mongol conquest, Asia
1490	Portuguese reach what is now Mozambique	**1346–1349** Black Death sweeps through Europe
c.1500	Shona people abandon Great Zimbabwe, move north and found new Mutapa dynasty	**1368** Ming dynasty rules, China
1500s–1700s	Tsonga create successive kingdoms of Nyaka, Tembe, and Maputo. They flourish in what is now Mozambique	**1492** Christopher Columbus reaches Americas

1501–1800

1511	Portuguese discover uninhabited Mauritius	**1519–1522** Ferdinand Magellan sails around the world
1590s	Dutch trading ships stop for supplies at the Cape, South Africa; Dutch settle Mauritius	**1521** Spain conquers Aztecs
1652	Dutch East India Company sets up station at the Cape	**1526** Mughal Empire founded, India
1657	Some Dutch East India Company soldiers become farmers, later known as Boers	**1619** First African slaves arrive Jamestown, Virginia
1657–1677	Boers seize land from Khoikhoi leading to conflict; Khoikhoi defeated	**1620** Mayflower reaches New England, North America
1710	Dutch abandon Mauritius; French occupy the island in 1715	**c. 1760** Industrial Revolution begins, Britain
1795	Ngakawetse chiefdom, central Botswana	**1776–1783** American Revolution
1795–1799	Boers unsuccessfully rebel against Cape authority	**1789–1799** French Revolution
1799–1878	Xhosa and Boers fight series of nine wars; Boers fail to defeat Xhosa who are ultimately defeated by British	
1797	Merina kingdom established in Madagascar	

1801–1850

1806	British take Cape Colony from Dutch; Cape and Mauritius become British colonies	**1804** Napoleon becomes emperor of France
1815	Nguni kingdoms of Ndwandwe, Ngwane, and Mthethwa dominate Natal region, South Africa	**1815** Napoleon defeated at Battle of Waterloo
1816	Shaka becomes Zulu leader	**1816–1828** Chile, Venezuela, Brazil, Argentina, Peru and
1818–1819	Zulu-Ndwandwe war confirms Zulu supremacy, Natal	

SOUTHERN AFRICAN EVENTS	WORLD EVENTS
1819–1839 *Mfecane/Difaqane* period: mass migrations and wars, South Africa	Uruguay became independent from Spain and Portugal
1820 5,000 British emigrate to Cape Colony, South Africa	**1821–1830** Greek war of independence
1820s Ndebele kingdom founded, Highveld, South Africa	**1846–1848** US–Mexican War
1824 Moshoeshoe I founds Basotho kingdom, Lesotho	**1848** Marx and Engels publish *Communist Manifesto*
1830s Ngoni state, Gaza, emerges, modern Mozambique	
1831 Sotho defeat invading Ndebele	
1835–1848 Boers undertake Great Trek. They encounter and fight Ndebele and Zulu	
1837 Ndebele migrate north to modern Zimbabwe where they become Matebele	
1838 Battle of Blood River: Boers defeat Zulu	
1841 Mayotte becomes French colony, Comoros	
1839–1865 Mswati I creates powerful Swazi nation	

1851–1900

SOUTHERN AFRICAN EVENTS	WORLD EVENTS
1851–1852 Sotho-British wars	**1861** Unification of Italy complete
1852 Boers found South African Republic, later Transvaal	**1861–1865** US Civil War
1854 Boers found Orange Free State	**1868** Meiji restoration, Japan
1855 Basuto kingdom reaches height	**1869** Suez Canal opens
1860–1867 Venda and Sotho drive Boers from lands north of Olifants River	**1871** Germany unified
1865–1868 Basotho becomes British colony of Basutoland	**1898** Spanish-American War
1867 Diamonds found Vaal Valley	
1868 Gold rush begins, Tati Valley, South Africa	
1871 British annex diamond fields, South Africa	
1877 British annex Transvaal	
1879 British defeat Pedi and Zulu	
1880–1881 "Gun War": Sotho rebel against British; Transvaal Boers rebel against British rule	
1883–1884 British partition Zululand leading to civil war	
1883–1885 Franco-Merina War, Madagascar	
1884–1885 British create Bechuanaland colony over Tswana; Comoros becomes French colony	
1884 Germans colonize South West Africa, modern Namibia	
1886 Gold rush begins Witwatersrand; Johannesburg founded, South Africa	
1890 British South Africa Company (BSAC) colonizes Southern Rhodesia	
1894 Swaziland becomes British colony	
1895 French colonize Madagascar	
1899–1902 Anglo-Boer War: British defeat Boers	

1901–1950

SOUTHERN AFRICAN EVENTS	WORLD EVENTS
1904–1905 Herero uprising, South West Africa, put down brutally	**1904–1905** Russo-Japanese War
1906 Bambatha rebellion	**1905** First Russian Revolution
1910 White-ruled Union of South Africa formed from British Cape and Natal colonies and Boer republics. It is a British dominion.	**1914–1918** World War I
	1917 Second Russian Revolution; communists in power
1912 Afrikaner National Party formed, South Africa. South African Native National Congress (SANNC) formed	**1929** Wall Street Crash leads to economic depression

Colonial occupation and independence

SOUTHERN AFRICAN EVENTS	WORLD EVENTS
1914–1918 World War I: German colonies transferred to South Africa	**1939–1945** World War II
1920 Zululand joins South Africa	**1946** United Nations (UN) formed
1923 SANNC becomes African National Party (ANC)	**1949** Communists gain power in China
1928 Inkatha, Zulu nationalist movement, founded	**1949** North Atlantic Treaty Organization (NATO) formed
1939–1945 World War II: manufacturing expands, South Africa.	**1950–1953** Korean War
1944 ANC Youth League formed	
1948 Nationalist government, South Africa, introduces apartheid. Series of repressive laws follow.	

1951–1970

1952 Defiance Campaign against apartheid laws	**1954** Algerian war of independence begins against France
1953 White-ruled Central African Federation (CAF) formed: Southern and Northern Rhodesia and Nyasaland	**1955** Warsaw Pact set up in eastern Europe
1956–61 Treason Trial, South Africa	**1959** Fidel Castro leads Cuban revolution
1960 South West African People's Organization (SWAPO) formed	**1962** Cuban missile crisis
1960 Sharpeville Massacre, South Africa	**1963** John F. Kennedy assassinated
1960 Madagascar achieves independence from France; *Frente de Libertaçao de Moçambique* (FRELIMO) launched	**1965–1973** US troops fight in Vietnam
1962 Zimbabwe African People's Union (ZAPU) formed, Southern Rhodesia	**1967** Six-Day War between Israel and Egypt and other Arab nations
1963 Zimbabwe African National Union (ZANU) formed	**1967–1970** Biafran civil war, Nigeria
1964 Nelson Mandela and other ANC leaders imprisoned	**1969** Neil Armstrong lands on the moon
1965 White-minority regime illegally declares Northern Rhodesia independent as Rhodesia	
1966 SWAPO rebels confront South African forces	
1966 Lesotho independent; Botswana independent	
1967–75 Guerrilla warfare against white rule in Rhodesia	
1968 Mauritius and Swaziland independent	

1971–1980

1971 UN declares South Africa's occupation of South West Africa illegal	**1973** Arabs ban oil sales to US causing worldwide oil crisis
1972 Military takeover in Madagascar	**1973** Yom Kippur War between Egypt and Israel
1973 King of Swaziland assumes absolute power	**1979** Islamic fundamentalists seize power, Iran
1975 FRELIMO forms government in Mozambique; *Resistência National Mocambicana* (Renamo) rebels begin civil war	**1979** USSR invades Afghanistan
1975 Mozambique and Comoros independent	**1980–1988** Iran-Iraq war
1976 Soweto uprising; police fire on schoolchildren	
1976 Black Africans; ZAPU and ZANU join to form Patriotic Front (PF), Rhodesia	
1978 South Africa bombs SWAPO refugee camp	
1979 Opposition parties banned, Lesotho	
1980 Zimbabwe independent; white-minority rule	

1981–2002

1981 South African government launches military force against ANC offices, Mozambique	**1982–1985** Israel invades Lebanon
1982 Deaths follow Inkatha uprising in Boipatong	

SOUTHERN AFRICAN EVENTS

1986	Military coup in Lesotho; State of Emergency declared after rioting in townships
1986	Mandela talks with South African government
1990	Nelson Mandela released from prison; ANC and other groups unbanned
1990	Namibia achieves independence
1991	Zimbabwe abandons one-party system; apartheid officially ends in South Africa
1992	Civil war ends in Mozambique; security forces massacred Boipatong, South Africa
1993	Elections held Madagascar; civilian rule returns, Lesotho
1994	First multiracial elections, South Africa. ANC wins elections with Nelson Mandela as president.
1995	Moshoeshoe II becomes king of Lesotho; military coup, Comoros
1996–1998	Truth and Reconciliation Committee, South Africa, aims to heal divisions
2002	Robert Mugabe re-elected Zimbabwe's president

WORLD EVENTS

1989	Revolution in Romania
1990	East and West Germany re-united
1990–1991	Gulf War follows Iraqi invasion of Kuwait
1991	Break up of Soviet Union; communism collapses in USSR and eastern Europe
1992	End of Cold War
1994–1996	Civil war, Rwanda; conflict spreads to Burundi
1998	Good Friday Agreement, peace in Northern Ireland
2001	Terrorist attack on World Trade Center, New York. Americans invade Afghanistan
2002	Israeli-Arab conflict

COLONIAL OCCUPATION AND INDEPENDENCE

Country	Independence	Occupied*	Colonial power
Botswana *as (Bechuanaland)*	Sept 30, 1966	1885	Britain
Comoros	July 6, 1975	1843	France
Lesotho *(as Basutoland)*	Oct 4, 1966	1868	Britain
Madagascar	June 26, 1960	1895	France
Mauritius	March 12, 1968	1715	France 1715–1810; Britain 1810–1968
Mozambique	June 25, 1975	1505	Portugal
Namibia *(as South West Africa)*	March 21, 1990	1884	Germany 1884–1919; occupied by South Africa 1915–90
Swaziland	Sept 6, 1968	1894	Britain (administered by the Boer's South African Republic 1894–1902)
Zimbabwe *(as Southern Rhodesia then Rhodesia)*	April 18, 1980	1890	Britain

*The years given for the beginning of occupation by the modern-day nations are those by which a significant area of coastal and hinterland territory had been occupied by a colonial power.

Independence
The two stamps above were issued to commemorate independence in Lesotho in 1966 (top) and in Namibia in 1990 (bottom).

© DIAGRAM

17

Hunting ostriches
Remains of weapons, tools, and animal bones help to give people in modern times a view of prehistoric life in Southern Africa.

Fossil finds
The map shows the five main sites in Southern Africa where fossils of early humans have been found.

Southern Africa's prehistory begins many thousands of years ago. Archaeologists – people who study remains of prehistoric peoples – have found evidence of hominids, early human-like creatures. They were probably australopithecines, upright walking creatures, who were the earliest human ancestors. They roamed the highland plains of southern Africa some 3–1 million years ago. Gradually, they evolved into more developed species: *Homo habilis* and *Homo erectus*, who collected fruits and berries, and used simple technology, based on stone tools, such as axes and choppers

Prehistoric humans

The earliest known evidence of modern humans, or *Homo sapiens*, dates back at least 100,000 years. Archaeologists have found fossils associated with early humans in the Klasies River Mouth Cave, in the eastern Cape of South Africa, that are between 120,000 and 80,000 years old. They have also found fossils in the Border Cave on the South African-Swaziland border that date back some 90,000 years. Few skeletons survive but archaeologists have found remains of tools, animal bones, fireplaces, and shelters that have helped them to build up a picture of the prehistoric peoples of Southern Africa.

A village settlement
A father and son return to their village after hunting, while other members of the settlement sort and prepare fruits for eating using simple tools.

© DIAGRAM

Ancestors

Some ancient bones found in South Africa show similarities to the Khoisan and Bantu-speaking peoples of today. The skull (top left) was found at Florisbad and is more than 200,000 years old. Khoisan skulls (middle left), with small noses and ears, were discovered perhaps 40,000 years ago. The first fossils resembling today's Bantu-speakiers were found in sub-Saharan Africa about 20,000 years ago (bottom left).

The first known inhabitants of Southern Africa were the Khoikhoi and the closely related San. There is much debate about their origins but some scholars believe that they evolved in the dry grasslands of the northern Kalahari desert, in what is now Botswana, and spread outwards to Namibia and the Cape. Over many hundreds of years, the Khoikhoi, who were not black Africans, but made up a unique grouping, were absorbed into the larger Khoisan ethnic group. Today, they are remembered mainly as a historical ethnic group. Small numbers of San, descendants of these early people, still survive in parts of Botswana and Namibia.

A simple counting device

The remnants of the lower leg bones of baboons were found in Border Cave in South Africa. Notches were carved into the bones at regular intervals suggesting that the bones may have been used as a means of counting.

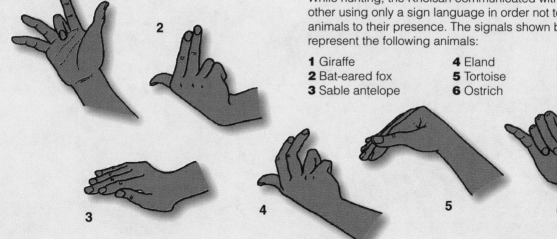

Silent communication

While hunting, the Khoisan communicated with each other using only a sign language in order not to alert the animals to their presence. The signals shown below represent the following animals:

1 Giraffe
2 Bat-eared fox
3 Sable antelope
4 Eland
5 Tortoise
6 Ostrich

Khoisan

The Khoisan, who were descendants of the early Khoikhoi and San, probably came from what are now western Zimbabwe and northern Botswana. At least 20,000 years ago they were living in small bands, at some distance from each other. They were hunter-gatherers. Instead of growing crops and farming, they collected, or gathered, fruits, nuts, berries, and other plants, and hunted a range of animals.

The San were particularly skilled hunters. Evidence found in caves by archaeologists of animal bones and other remains indicate that the San probably tracked and hunted smaller animals, such as rodents and rabbits, which they caught in traps. They also stalked larger animals, including hippos, rhinos, and elephants, which they killed with bows and arrows.

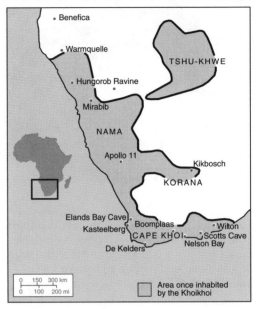

Birthplace (above)
Remains of livestock and pottery found at the named places suggest that the Khoikhoi may once have inhabited these (tinted) areas in Southern Africa.

Old customs die hard (below)
Some Khoisan still hunt with bows and arrows today in the manner practiced by their Paleolithic ancestors.

© DIAGRAM

A funeral relic
Painted by a Khoisan artist, and excavated from Coldstream Cave on the southern Cape coast, this stone was found on the shoulder of a skeleton and probably played a role in funeral rites of the time.

For many generations the Khoisan lived a nomadic or semi-nomadic existence. They lived in groups consisting of between 25–50 people, all related to each other biologically or through marriage. The groups did not have a formal system of government; instead, there were leaders rather than rulers. Groups made decisions through discussion and consensus, shared their property, and divided food and water according to seniority.

The Khoisan lived in rock shelters and caves, or made brushwood shelters when they were on the move. For survival, they relied on materials in their immediate surroundings from plants through to stones and sticks. Their technology reflected their needs. They used pointed digging sticks for gathering plants, and fashioned a large number of stone tools.

Skilled artists

The Khoisan are well known for the beauty and excellence of their rock paintings, some of which still survive in what are now Zimbabwe, Botswana, and the Drakensberg Mountains. A famous site is Apollo 11 Cave, in southern Namibia, where cave paintings survive that date back to about 27,000 BCE. Rock paintings there are the earliest known examples and give us a clear picture of how the Khoisan hunted and fished.

Gathering roots and bulbs
The main tool used was a digging stick. Tapered at one end, a circular stone weight was placed as far down the stick as possible. The other end of the stick was sharpened to a point. The gatherer then used the weighted tool for prising roots and bulbs from the parched earth.

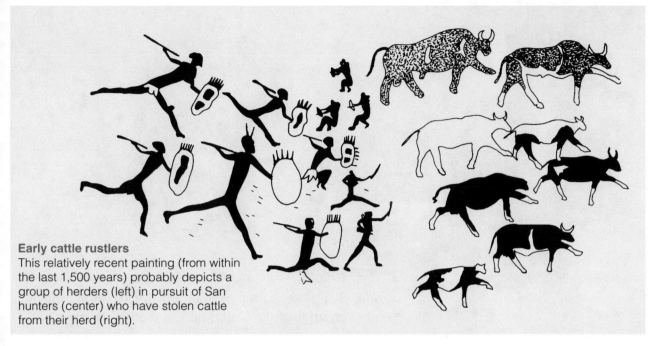

Early cattle rustlers
This relatively recent painting (from within the last 1,500 years) probably depicts a group of herders (left) in pursuit of San hunters (center) who have stolen cattle from their herd (right).

Farming people

The San remained hunter-gatherers but, at some point, some hunter-gatherers in northern Botswana began to keep animals. Over generations, they made their way south, reaching the Cape about 2,000 years ago. There some developed into pastoralists – people who raise and herd cattle – grazing fat-tailed sheep and long-horned cattle. The Khoisan continued to gather plants and hunt animals, but their lives became more settled and they had new sources of food, including milk. Those who lived on the coast fished and gathered shell food.

The pastoral Khoisan, who were mainly Khoikhoi, lived in larger, more settled communities, consisting of between 10 to 40 dome-shaped dwellings. Each community or settlement contained as many as 100–200 people. They developed a more settled farming existence, and by the time Europeans arrived some 1500 years later, were well-established farming people.

Engraved eggshells
The Khoisan have for centuries used ostrich eggshells for storing water (and even food). This highly-decorated example dates from the 20th century.

© DIAGRAM

The new arrivals

A warm shelter
Members of one of the San groups set up camp in a semi-desert region of Southern Africa.

Great changes occurred in Southern Africa during the early centuries of the Common Era. Settled farming communities were established, new technologies were introduced, and a number of wealthy trading centers and states emerged.

The Iron Age

BCE

c. 500 Khoisan-speaking hunter-gatherers, using stone tools, inhabit Southern Africa

c. 200–150 People keep sheep and make pottery

CE

c.180–200 Farming community at Mabveni.

200s Bantu-speaking peoples begin arriving in Southern Africa

c.200 Bantu-speaking herders and ironworkers move into Mozambique region

c.300 Bantu-speaking farmers enter what is now Lesotho from the north. They displace hunter-gatherers living there.

300s–400s Bantu-speakers arrive in north and southeast Southern Africa

400s Indonesian settlers live on Comoros Islands

400s Bantu-speaking peoples settle Zimbabwe region

c. 420 Earliest dated evidence of farming and ironworking, Botswana

700–1300 Toutswe tradition: cattle-owning Iron-Age communities flourish in Botswana

700 First evidence of Muslim traders on coast at Chibuene

900s Mapungubwe trading center established on Limpopo River

1000s Bantu-speaking people migrate from mainland Southern Africa to island of Madagascar.

1000s Leopard Kopje, major Iron-Age settlement, built in Zimbabwe

c. 1100s Manekweni, in what is now Mozambique, develops as center for Indian Ocean gold trade

c. 1100 State centered on Great Zimbabwe develops

1100–1300 Mapungubwe trading center at peak of prosperity

c. 1300s Swahili merchants set up trading cities at Sofala and Chibuene

1300s–1400s Great Zimbabwe at height of power

1400s Bantu-speaking people migrate into Namibia area, displacing San

Stalking prey
The Khoisan were the first known inhabitants of Southern Africa, and they lived in widely-scattered bands. They were hunter-gatherers, and emerged in the dry grasslands of the northern Kalahari desert where they stalked animals before killing them with bows and arrows.

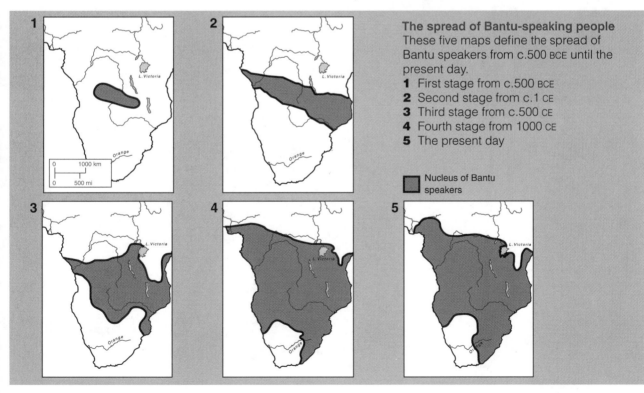

The spread of Bantu-speaking people
These five maps define the spread of Bantu speakers from c.500 BCE until the present day.
1 First stage from c.500 BCE
2 Second stage from c.1 CE
3 Third stage from c.500 CE
4 Fourth stage from 1000 CE
5 The present day

◻ Nucleus of Bantu speakers

© DIAGRAM

New technologies

Old tools
This remnant of either an old tool (or weapon) was discovered in Zimbabwe, and was probably produced by Bantu-speaking people.

Beginning in the first century CE, Bantu-speaking peoples, who absorbed or displaced most of the indigenous Khoikhoi and San peoples, began to arrive in Southern Africa. Their journeys through the region took several hundred years but, by the 1400s, Bantu-speakers had migrated as far as what is now known as Namibia. Today, most black Southern Africans are descended from those early Bantu people.

The Bantu-speakers probably originated in eastern Nigeria as long ago as 4,000 years. Initially, they spread over Central Africa and through the equatorial rainforest. Between about 500 BCE and 300 CE, they moved eastward and southward into East and Southern Africa. Bantu-speakers who came to Southern Africa included two main groups: the Nguni, who today include the Swazi, Xhosa, and Zulu, and the Tswana-Sotho, the ancestors of today's people of Botswana and Lesotho.

Old weapons
Found in Zimbabwe, this old weapon (or tool) is solid testimony to the flourishing trade in iron manufacture by the Bantu-speakers in Southern Africa.

Smelting iron
This traditional method of smelting iron in a furnace using bellows is still practiced by some tribes in Southern Africa today.

Migrations

Much is still unknown about the early Bantu migrations but it is probable they made two main migrations: east and west. Between the second and fifth centuries CE, eastern Bantu-speakers arrived in what are now southern Zimbabwe, eastern South Africa, Mozambique, and Swaziland. They were farmers who cultivated crops and, additionally, raised cattle on the coastal regions, by rivers, and in the valleys.

Western Bantu-speakers entered southwestern Zimbabwe, along the eastern edges of the Kalahari Desert, into what is now Botswana, and later into eastern South Africa and Mozambique. They also grew cereals, worked metal, and raised livestock.

Iron ax
This iron ax was discovered by European explorers in Southern Africa, and is believed to have been made by Zulu ironworkers.

A Lydenburg head
Named after the place in which it was discovered in the 1950s, this is one of seven terracotta heads now believed to be the earliest known form of sculpture in Southern Africa.

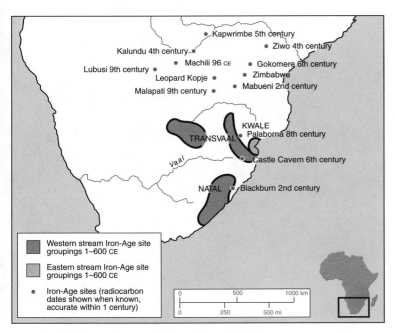

Kapwrimbe 5th century
Kalundu 4th century
Ziwo 4th century
Lubusi 9th century
Machili 96 CE
Gokomere 6th century
Leopard Kopje
Zimbabwe
Malapati 9th century
Mabueni 2nd century
KWALE
TRANSVAAL
Palaborna 8th century
Vaal
Castle Cavern 6th century
NATAL
Blackburn 2nd century

■ Western stream Iron-Age site groupings 1–600 CE

■ Eastern stream Iron-Age site groupings 1–600 CE

• Iron-Age sites (radiocarbon dates shown when known, accurate within 1 century)

0 — 500 — 1000 km
0 — 250 — 500 mi

Bantu metal technology
The eastern and western Bantu-speakers arrived in Southern Africa from 1–600 CE. Those in the east were farmers and cattle herders, while those in the west also practiced metalworking.

© DIAGRAM

27

The Bantu-speakers brought with them new farming techniques, such as the hoe. Most importantly, they introduced metal working (iron and copper) into Southern Africa. They were skilled iron workers, who smelted metal in clay kilns fuelled by wood charcoal. By the 300s CE, early farming communities, which used iron tools, had developed south of the Limpopo River, previously inhabited only by hunter-gatherers. Bantu-speaking farmers grew crops such as sorgum, millet, groundnuts, melons, and gourds, and herded sheep, goats, and cattle. They produced pottery, and used iron tools for turning the soil and harvesting.

Staple crops
Millet (above left) requires little rainfall to grow; sorghum (above right) requires more rainfall than millet, but withstands drought more successfully. They were both grown by the first Bantu-speakers in Southern Africa.

An important commodity
Bantu-speakers traded in iron (top) – valuable for making tools and weapons – after it had been smelted (bottom left) and forged (bottom right).

Toutswe culture

As time passed, permanent settlements appeared that were larger and more complex than previous communities. They used more sophisticated ironworking techniques, mined gold and copper, and created stone buildings. They also produced distinctive ceramics or pottery. Some communities developed into states or chiefdoms, with new forms of stratified social and political organization. They became important trading centers. One of the earliest was Toutswe, in what is now eastern Botswana, which first emerged about 700 CE. Other important centers included Mapungubwe on the Limpopo River, Manekweni, in what is now Mozambique, and Great Zimbabwe in what is now Zimbabwe.

Toutswe was an important center not far from the upper Limpopo valley. Consisting of a number of villages, it was a large cattle-keeping chiefdom. Most people lived in the valleys, with chiefs and other important rulers living on well defended hilltop capitals. Cattle was an increasingly source of wealth and the center contained large herds. Trade too was important, and archaeologists have found evidence that the Toutswe culture engaged in long-distance trade, probably with Muslim traders on the Indian Ocean.

The Toutswe culture reached its height between about 950-1050 but by about 1300 had gone into decline, probably because of overgrazing and drought. Other trading centers too also began to decline.

Glass beads
Toutswe was an important center in what is now eastern Botswana. Its trade was often long-distance. These beads probably came from lands around the Indian Ocean.

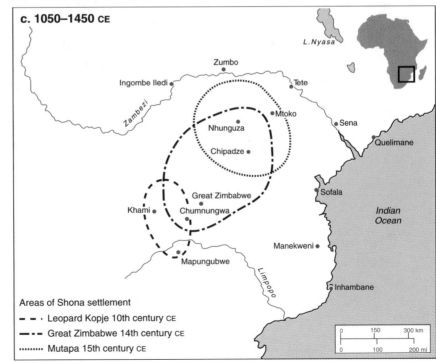

c. 1050–1450 CE

L.Nyasa
Zumbo
Ingombe Iledi
Tete
Zambezi
Mtoko
Sena
Nhunguza
Quelimane
Chipadze
Great Zimbabwe
Sofala
Khami
Chumnungwa
Indian Ocean
Manekweni
Mapungubwe
Limpopo
Inhambane

Areas of Shona settlement
– – · Leopard Kopje 10th century CE
–·– · Great Zimbabwe 14th century CE
········· Mutapa 15th century CE

0   150   300 km
0   100   200 mi

© DIAGRAM

Great trading centers
The Shona occupied the Zimbabwe plateau in the 10th century, which contained the three important trading centers of Mapungubwe, Manekeweni, and Great Zimbabwe.

Mapungubwe

One of the most important Iron-Age states in Southern Africa was Mapungubwe, which lay near where the borders of what are now South Africa, Botswana, and Zimbabwe converge. Originally a trading settlement, it developed into a centralized state based on gold mining and trade. The center of the kingdom was Bambandyalo, just south of the Limpopo River.

Mapungubwe was settled in about the 900s CE and flourished between 1100–1300 CE. Ongoing archaeological work has uncovered a great deal of information about the site. Mapungubwe was part of an extensive farming society, based on cattle. It was a highly stratified society with a wealthy and privileged political and bureaucratic elite who lived, separated from the ordinary people, on top of Mapungubwe hill. The commoners, or ordinary people, lived at the foot of the hill in a village settlement. Stone walls and passages separated the two areas. The wealthy elite built stone dwellings and controlled trade and cattle over a wide area that stretched from Botswana to Mozambique. They lived luxurious lives and, when they died, they were buried with gold and copper ornaments, beads, and imported pottery and cloth.

The people of Mapungubwe raised and kept cattle. Elephants roamed the Limpopo valley and evidence shows that the people also collected and worked ivory. The region was also rich in gold, which was deposited in the river beds. Skilled craftspeople made pottery objects and fine bone tools. Archaeological evidence also indicates that the people wove cloth.

Center of a kingdom
This map shows the original location of Mapungubwe. It lay near where the borders of what are now South Africa, Botswana, and Zimbabwe converge.

Trading links stretched from Mapungubwe to trading posts on the Indian Ocean from where Muslim traders shipped goods to Arabia and China. Archaeologists have uncovered evidence that shows Mapungubwe engaged in an extensive long-distance trade, exchanging goods such as ivory, gold, bone, and tortoiseshell for glass beads, cloth, and Chinese porcelain. Gold beads, bangles, bowls, figurines, and jewelry have also been found on the site.

During the 1200s, Mapungubwe began declining and the hill site had been abandoned by 1300. The reasons are uncertain. The area may not have been able to support such a large society, or environmental factors, such as drought or disease, may have brought the society to an end.

Coastal ports

Arab merchants set up trading posts on the eastern coast of Africa. By about 700 CE, Arabs had established Chibuene (Inhambane) on the Mozambique coast and others followed. One important trading port was Sofala, which traded in goods to and from Mozambique. At Chibuene, archeologists have found fragments of porcelain, and pieces of bottles which are probably Chinese, as well as examples of local pottery. Africans took goods, such as animal skins, ivory, gold, and copper, from centers such as Mapungubwe to the coast, from where they were shipped to Asia.

A rich legacy
Among the many impressive artifacts found at Mapungubwe were this golden ceremonial bowl and baton. The region, rich in gold, provided the raw material for the local craftworkers, and many of these ornamental items were buried with the wealthy elite who lived on top of Mapungubwe hill.

EMERGING STATES

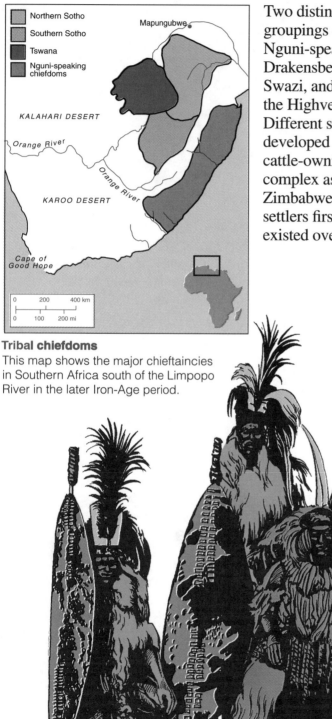

Northern Sotho
Southern Sotho
Tswana
Nguni-speaking chiefdoms

Mapungubwe

KALAHARI DESERT

Orange River

Orange River

KAROO DESERT

Cape of Good Hope

| 0 | 200 | 400 km |
| 0 | 100 | 200 mi |

Tribal chiefdoms
This map shows the major chieftaincies in Southern Africa south of the Limpopo River in the later Iron-Age period.

Two distinct cultural and linguistic Bantu-speaking groupings emerged in Southern Africa. They were the Nguni-speaking peoples who settled east of the Drakensberg Mountains, and included the Zulu, Ndebele, Swazi, and Xhosa, and the Sotho-Tswana, who settled on the Highveld, west of the Drakensberg Mountains. Different subgroups and clans emerged, many of which developed powerful kingdoms. Some were small-scale cattle-owning societies, based on kinship, and were not as complex as larger trading states, such as Toutswe or Great Zimbabwe, but by the mid-17th century, when Dutch settlers first began to arrive, chiefdoms and dynasties existed over most of Southern Africa.

Architect of a kingdom
King Mswati I, who reigned from 1839–1865, created a powerful Swazi kingdom when the region was under threat from colonial aggressors. He is shown here in full ceremonial dress with other similarly dressed Swazi chiefs.

Emerging states

200s	Nguni arrive in Southern Africa
900s–1200s	Muslims from East Africa settle northern Madagascar
c.1000	Sotho peoples arrive in the valleys of the Orange, Vaal, and Tugela rivers
c.1095	Tswana people migrate to area of modern Botswana
1100s	Muslim traders from East Africa settle on Comoros islands
c.1100	State centered on Great Zimbabwe develops
1100–1300	Mapungubwe trading center at peak of prosperity
c.1200	Great Enclosure built at Great Zimbabwe
c.1300s	Swahili merchants set up trading cities at Sofala and Chibuene
1300s–1400s	Great Zimbabwe at height of its prosperity
1400s	Bantu speakers migrate into region of modern Namibia
c.1400	Sotho establish main clans
c.1400	Torwa kingdom founded near present-day Bulawayo
c.1450–1500	Great Zimbabwe abandoned; Mutapa empire established to the north
1488	Portuguese reach what is now South Africa
1490	Portuguese reach what is now Mozambique
1500s–1700s	Successive Tsonga kingdoms: Nyaka, Tembe, and Maputo flourish in what is now Mozambique
1500	Diogo Dias, Portuguese navigator, is the first European to visit Madagascar
1510	Portuguese explore Mauritius
1590s	Dutch traders begin to stop at the Cape
1600s–1800s	Bapedi Empire of Pedi, Northern Sotho people
c.1600	Rozvi people conquer Torwa and set up Changamire state
1652	Dutch begin to settle Cape of Good Hope, South Africa

End of an empire

The British army defeated the Pedi, a Northern Sotho people, in 1879. This illustration graphically depicts Sekhukhuni, the king of the Pedi, being carried on a litter after the battle.

Soapstone bowl

A number of these bowls were found in the Lower Valley at Great Zimbabwe, and were probably used in ritualistic ceremonies aimed at contacting ancestors' spirits. This particular bowl depicts a procession of zebra, followed by a bird and a human-like figure leading a dog facing a baboon. The meaning remains a mystery to this day.

© DIAGRAM

Nguni and Ndebele

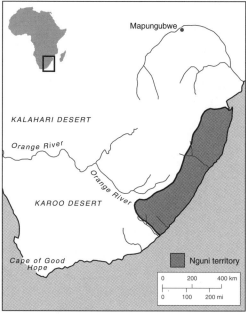

Where they lived

The tinted area of this map shows where the Nguni people lived c.1790. The northern part of the coast was occupied by the Ndebele, one of the many ethnic groups descended from the Nguni.

Nguni chiefdoms

The Nguni were the dominant Bantu language group east of the Drakensberg Mountains. They possibly originated from the Tsonga of Mozambique but less is known about their chiefdoms than those of the Sotho-Tswana. Before the 1700s, the Nguni, who were cattle-owning people, did not live in centralized states like the Sotho-Tswana, but instead settled in small, clan-based, village homesteads. A group of linked homesteads made up a chieftaincy.

By the 1700s, Nguni chiefdoms stretched from the Usutu River southward to the Sunday River. Most were small but larger, more powerful chiefdoms were emerging. They included the Xhosa, Thembu, Mpondo, Zizi, Hlubi, Mthethwa, Ndwandwe, Ngwane (the forerunner of the great Swazi nation), and Zulu.

Ndebele

The Ndebele were one of the many ethnic groups who descended from the original Nguni settlers. In the late 1500s the Ndebele split off from the Nguni under a chief called Musi. Soon afterward, the Ndebele split into two groups, Northern and Southern, most of whom migrated from what is now Natal into the Transvaal where northern Ndebele were absorbed by their Sotho neighbors.

A Xhosa leader
During his lifetime (1779–1829) Ngquika saw the territory occupied by the Xhosa lost to Europeans. He had also to contend with opposition from within the Xhosa nation itself.

Nguni homesteads

The average Nguni house was made from a mixture of grass and reeds, woven together and tied to a central pole. Cattle, an integral part of the Nguni livelihood, were kept in a circular *kraal* (enclosure for animals), around which the houses were situated. The people lived in separate family homesteads which were scattered around the countryside. A chieftaincy consisted of a group of related homesteads.

© DIAGRAM

Sotho-Tswana chiefdoms

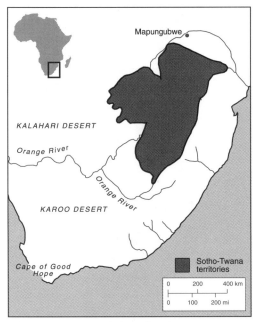

A number of powerful Sotho-Tswana chiefdoms emerged in the 18th century, controlling particular territories and setting up states on the Highveld. They developed complex social and political structures, particularly in the central and western areas. A chief or king was head of state, ruling over a large capital city containing between 15,000–20,000 people by the late 1700s. The Sotho-Tswana chiefdoms cultivated cereals and other crops, such as pumpkins and beans, in fields close to the town. Large herds of cattle grazed on the veld and beyond the cattle were hunting grounds. Many chiefdoms also produced iron and copper. State capitals were divided into administrative districts or wards, each of which consisted of related families and was ruled by a headman. When a kingdom expanded, it absorbed new chiefdoms.

Where they lived (above)
The tinted area of this map of shows where the Sotho-Tswana people lived c.1790.

Sotho-Tswana clans

The Sotho and Tswana language groups were closely related. By the 1000s CE the Sotho had settled on the Highveld – the high, dry plains to the west of the Drakensberg Mountains – and in the valleys of the Orange, Vaal, and Tugela rivers. By about 1400, different clans had emerged, each of which took a particular animal for its symbol or totem. The Kwene, for instance, took the crocodile as their totem. Clan groups came together to form three main divisions: the Northern Sotho, Southern Sotho, and the Tswana, also known as the Western Sotho, later the people of Botswana.

Friend or foe?
Clan groups within the Sotho-Tswana often adopted creatures as their symbol or totem; the Kwene clan, for example, chose the crocodile.

A Sotho compound
Among the Sotho, circular houses with stone or wicker walls, and conically-shaped thatched roofs, were linked together to form a compound (left). Traditional Tswana houses were circular in shape, with mud or stone walls, and had a thatched roof which was supported by rafters (below).

Toy cattle
Many children from cattle-rearing families used toys of this kind to play games in which they imitated their parents' daily work with the herds.

© DIAGRAM

37

The western clans

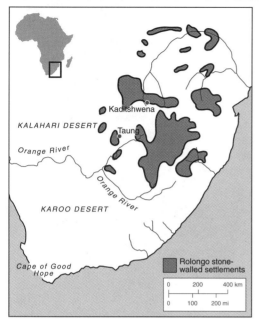

Evidence from the past
Aerial photographs of Southern Africa reveal stone-walled settlements, dating from the 16th–19th centuries, which were built by the western clans such as the Rolong.

One of the most powerful of the western clans was the Rolong, whose founding ancestor is thought to have lived around 1300 CE. The Rolong dominated a region that stretched north from the Kalahari Desert southward to the Vaal River. They kept large cattle herds and controlled access to local iron ore deposits. By the 1700s, they had established a powerful kingdom and traded with the Khoisan in the south and Bantu-speakers as far as northern Namibia. Their most famous ruler was Tau, still remembered in oral traditions as a great military ruler. The Rolong built large towns with stone walls, including their capital Taung. After Tau's death, his successors formed further subdivisions, one of which, the Thlaping, established an independent state.

Another powerful group, were the Hurutshe, whose descendants now live in Botswana. Living to the east of the Rolong, they controlled the hill country around the headwaters of the Eland and Marico rivers. They worked iron and copper, built stone-walled enclosures, and traded with surrounding people. More than 15,000 people lived in the Hurutshe capital, Kaditshwena.

Linked closely to them were the Kwena who crossed the Vaal River sometime between 1550–1650 and eventually founded the kingdom of Lesotho. By the late 1600s, their chiefdoms stretched north of the Hurutshe from what is now Pretoria to Molepolole.

The Kgatla controlled the northeast central region of what is now the Transvaal. From them came several powerful groups such as the Pedi. During the 1600s the Pedi group of clans dominated the Northern Sotho. They moved northeastward to the Olifants River region of the northern Drakensberg and built up a powerful state – the Bapedi Empire – which lasted for two hundred years.

Venda and Lobedu

Two important groups, not part of the Sotho-Tswana complex, were the Venda and Lobedu. During the 1600s, the Venda, led by Thoho Ya Ndou, crossed the Limpopo River and entered what is now Transvaal. They smelted and exported copper and ivory and were skilled archers, which gave them military supremacy. For a while, they controlled much of the eastern region of Southern Africa.

Special drum
Ngoma drums, which are hemispherical in shape and elaborately decorated, are only used in the courts of Venda headmen. It was believed that the very first Venda leaders possessed an *ngoma* drum.

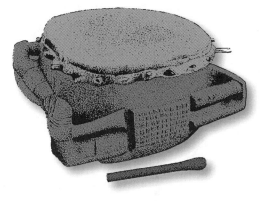

Three clan leaders
The Sotho had established their main clans on the Highveld west of the Drakensberg Mountains in Southern Africa by c.1400. Moshoeshoe (far left) was widely credited with being a direct descendant of the founder of the Sotho nation. Mashopa (center) was the third son of Moshoeshoe and became leader of the Southern Sotho. He fought against both Africans and Afrikaners and, in the 1870s, he opposed the Cape administration in Basutoland. Sekhukhuni (left) was the king of the Pedi peoples, and led them in their war against the Boers in the 1860s.

© DIAGRAM

Great Zimbabwe: a sophisticated civilization

Where it was

The Zimbabwe plateau was occupied in the 10th century by the Shona people. They rebuilt the original site from the mid-14th century, then abandoned it c.1450.

For 400 years, between the 12th and 16th centuries, a remarkable civilization flourished in the southeast of what is now Zimbabwe. It was called Great Zimbabwe and was the political, religious, and commercial center of a prosperous Shona civilization. Today, massive stone walls still stand imposingly on the hilltop site, not far from the present day town of Masvingo, as reminders of the once-great complex.

Shona architects

Originally Iron-Age farmers, the Shona arrived on the Zimbabwean plateau in about the 10th century. They developed a sophisticated civilization, building dry-wall enclosures as palaces for their kings and chiefs. The enclosures were known as zimbabwes *(literally, stone houses). The Shona may have built as many as 200 — remains of their palaces stretch from southeast Zimbabwe into Mozambique — but the largest and most imposing was Great*

Zimbabwe. The Shona began building their enclosures in the late 1100s. They did not use mortar (cement), and the quality of their stonework, particularly at Great Zimbabwe, was so excellent that for many years people believed that indigenous Africans could not have created the buildings.

Buildings and stonemasons

Covering an area of some 60 acres (24 hectares), Great Zimbabwe stood on a hilltop about 350 ft (100 m) above the surrounding plains. It consisted of massive stone walls, up to 30 ft (9 m) high and some 16 ft (5 m) thick at the base. The walls, which stood in carefully prepared trenches, enclosed a number of large, circular buildings made of mud and roofed with thatch. The buildings were 30 ft (9 m) or more in diameter, and about 20 ft (6 m) in height; some were divided into separate rooms.

To create the building blocks, Shona stonemasons built fires around boulders or granite outcrops, heated them up, then threw cold water onto the hot rock. The impact of the sudden cooling split the rock into stone slabs some 3–7 in (7.5–17 cm) thick. The masons then dragged the slabs to the site on sledges, and hammered and chiseled them into smaller blocks for building.

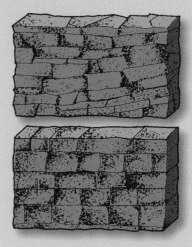

Developing skills
These two examples of stonework from Great Zimbabwe show how much more advanced the masons became over a period of years. The stone in the lower example is later, and more finely fitted, than the upper example.

© DIAGRAM

Great Zimbabwe: from wealth to decline

The wealth of the Shona came from farming, gold, and long-distance trade, and it was their prosperity which enabled them to build Great Zimbabwe, their capital, and major commercial and political center. Archeological evidence gathered in the last 50 years has shown that the people of Great Zimbabwe grew crops, mined gold and copper found on the Zimbabwean plateau, and traded gold and copper goods with coastal ports on the Mozambique coast. A wealthy elite controlled the trade routes, which stretched from the African interior through to Arab and Swahili ports, such as Sofala and Chibuene. Great Zimbabwe exported gold, copper, and ivory, and imported goods, such as silk and porcelain from China, glass beads from Indonesia, and highly-glazed porcelain from Persia (what is now Iran).

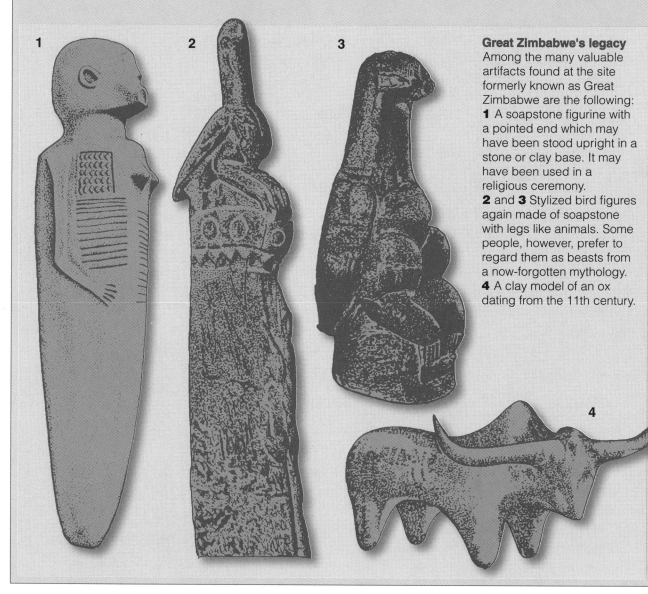

Great Zimbabwe's legacy

Among the many valuable artifacts found at the site formerly known as Great Zimbabwe are the following:
1 A soapstone figurine with a pointed end which may have been stood upright in a stone or clay base. It may have been used in a religious ceremony.
2 and **3** Stylized bird figures again made of soapstone with legs like animals. Some people, however, prefer to regard them as beasts from a now-forgotten mythology.
4 A clay model of an ox dating from the 11th century.

The end of Great Zimbabwe

From about 1450 Great Zimbabwe went into decline and its political importance came to an end. By 1500 the Shona kings had left Great Zimbabwe and moved their capital northward to a site on the Zambezi River. There a new Shona dynasty emerged — the Mwene Mutapas, who conquered a huge territory from the Kalahari Desert to the Indian Ocean. In the southwest, Great Zimbabwe's successor was Torwa, later succeeded by the Rozwi Changamire dynasty.

Great Zimbabwe continued as a religious and ritual center, focused on the worship of the Shona god Mwari, until the early part of the 19th century. In the 1830s the site was completely abandoned when Nguni refugees escaping from the social upheaval, known as the Mfecane, drove out the inhabitants or imprisoned them. Europeans arrived during the late 19th century and Great Zimbabwe's remaining riches were stolen or melted down.

A new Shona dynasty
Nyatsimba Mutoto (c.1440–c.1450) was founder of the Mwene Mutapa dynasty.

Cultural heritage (right)
The display of pots in Shona homes celebrated the household, marriage, and the woman's central role in these institutions. This Shona pot was made in 1960 and shows the tradition is still very much alive nowadays.

Local currency (below)
Copper ingots were used as currency in Great Zimbabwe, some of which were discovered as far away as China.

© DIAGRAM

EUROPEAN SETTLEMENT

The first Europeans to make contact with Southern Africa were the Portuguese navigators who, in the late 15th century, sailed around the Cape of Good Hope. The Dutch and British soon followed.

Early arrivals

During the early 1500s the Portuguese arrived in what is now Mozambique. They sacked the port of Sofala and began to settle on the eastern coast, taking over the gold trade that had been dominated by Arabs since the 10th century. Later they traded in slaves captured by the Tsonga people, who had founded kingdoms in the southeast. The Portuguese also explored the island of Mauritius but did not settle.

In the 1590s, Dutch traders began to use the Cape as a port to re-supply ships of the Dutch East India Company en route from Holland to the East. They encountered and bartered with the local Khoikhoi, exchanging iron, copper, beads, tobacco, and brandy for cattle and sheep, which they needed for provisions.

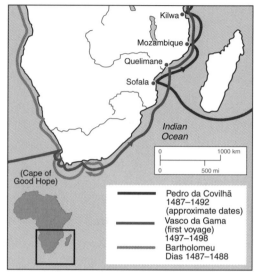

Voyages of discovery
This map shows the most important voyages around Southern Africa made by three Portuguese explorers from 1487–1498.

Bartering for food
This illustration, based on a 17th-century engraving, depicts European traders buying livestock from the Khoikhoi at the Cape. As well as cattle and sheep, minerals, beads, tobacco, and brandy were also traded between the two groups.

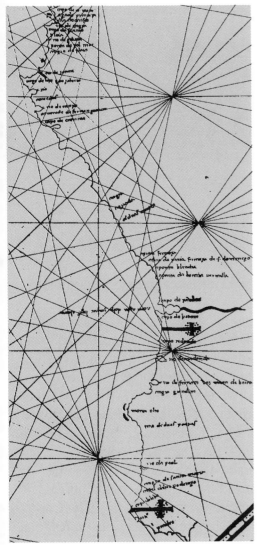

Settlement in Southern Africa

1488	Portuguese reach southern tip of Africa
1490	Portuguese reach Mozambique
1500	Portuguese navigator, Diogo Dias, visits Madagascar
1505	Portuguese sack Sofala
1508	French found city of Moçambique (Mozambique)
1510	Portuguese explore Mauritius
1531	Portuguese move inland along Zambezi River, Mozambique
1590s	Dutch traders begin to stop at the Cape
1598	Dutch claim Mauritius
c.1600	Rozwi people conquer Torwa; set up Changamire state, Zimbabwe
early 1700s	Dutch and English explore coast of what is now Namibia
1628	Portuguese missionaries introduce Christianity to Karanga peoples, Mozambique
1652	Dutch set up garrison at Cape of Good Hope
1657	Some Dutch soldiers become farmers (Boers) and come into conflict with Khoikhoi over cattle
1657–1677	Boers and Khoikhoi fight over land ownership
1693–1695	Changamire peoples attack Portuguese, Mozambique
1710	Dutch abandon Mauritius
1722	French colonize Mauritius
1770	Boers fight Xhosa
1773	Dutch claim Walvis Bay
1779–1878	Xhosa wars end with Xhosa losing their lands
1795	Ngakawetse chiefdom dominates central Botswana and British occupy Cape Colony
1795–1799	Boers rebel against Cape authorities
1806	Britain annexes Cape Colony
1807	Britain bans slave trade
1814	Dutch cede Cape Colony to Britain
1819–1839	*Mfecane*: period of mass migrations and wars
1820	First British settlers arrive Cape Colony
1832	Portugal bans system of land grants, Mozambique
1833	Britain ends slavery in British colonies
1835–1848	The Great Trek: Boers leave Cape Colony and trek inland
1838	Battle of Blood River: Boers defeat Zulu
1839	Boers establish Natalia republic (Natal)
1843	France annexes Mayotte, Comoros Islands
1843	Britain seizes Natal
1852	Boers establish South African Republic
1854	Boers set up Orange Free State (OFS)

Portuguese exploration
This is a detail from a Portuguese naval map, made in 1490, that represents the West African coast.

Bartholomeu Dias
He was a Portuguese explorer who sailed south of the Congo, then around the Cape of Good Hope in 1487. Dias later helped to prepare for Vasco da Gama's voyage around the African coast.

©DIAGRAM

Monopoly
In 1602 the Dutch republic granted the Dutch
East India Company (*Verenigde Oostindishe
Compagnie*, or VOC), the largest of its kind,
a monopoly on trade in the East Indies.

A Dutch colony in Southern Africa
Realizing both its economic and strategic
importance, the Dutch sent Jan van
Riebeeck to establish a colony at the Cape of
Good Hope in1652.

In 1652 Jan van Riebeeck, of the Dutch East India
Company, together with 125 men, set up a garrison and
supply station at the Cape, on the site of what is now
Cape Town. It soon grew into a permanent and much
larger settlement.

In 1657 the Company released some soldiers from their
contracts, allowing them to cultivate the land, herd cattle
and set up farms to provide food for the Company. They
later became known as Boers, after the Dutch word for
"farmers." Their children, those born in Africa, took the
name Afrikaners (Africans) after the Afrikaans language
– a simplified form of Dutch mixed with Bantu, Khoisan,
Portuguese and Malay – that they developed.

More Dutch immigrants followed, as well as some
French and Germans, and established settlements at
Stellenbosch (1679) and Drakenstein (1687). The Cape
settlers used slave labor, shipping in slaves from Angola,
Benin, and later Madagascar and Mozambique, but the
Company prohibited the use of local people.

However, as the Boers expanded their farms, they
increasingly encroached on the Khoikhoi, seizing their
cattle and grazing lands, and displacing the Khoikhoi
who, although technically not slaves, were forced to labor
for the Boers as servants and farm workers. Some
Khoikhoi reverted to being hunter-gatherers; many died
from diseases brought by the Europeans.

Some interbreeding took place between Europeans and
Khoikhoi, or Europeans and African slaves, resulting in
mixed-race descendants, later known as Cape Coloreds.

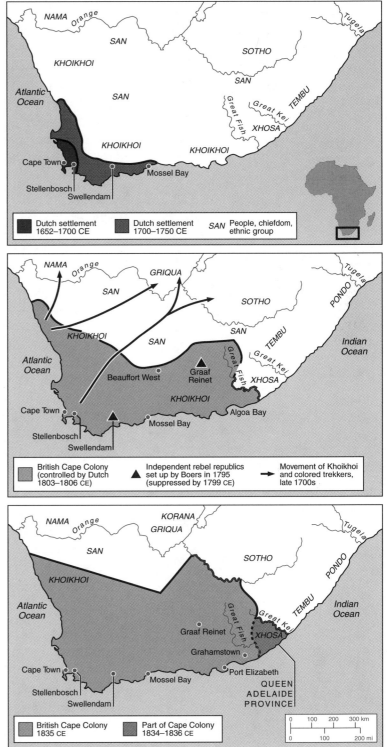

A Khoikoi settlement (above)

When the Dutch arrived in South Africa they found Khoikhoi communities. These generally consisted of extended clans, sometimes of up to 200 people. Some communities grazed herds of livestock on pastures near the settlements, so enabling them to feed large groups. Other Khoikhoi were hunter-gatherers.

The move toward independence (right)

Cape Colony was originally founded by the Dutch as a port to resupply European ships sailing to India, China and Southeast Asia. It gradually expanded in size during the period 1652–1750 (top map).The British seized control of the Cape from the Dutch in 1795, but gave it back eight years later in 1803. In 1806 the British annexed the colony (center map). By 1835 the British-controlled Cape Colony had expanded (bottom map). In 1910, it became a province, the Cape of Good Hope, in the Union of South Africa. In 1994, the province was divided into three: the Eastern, Northern, and Western Capes.

© DIAGRAM

Boer movements

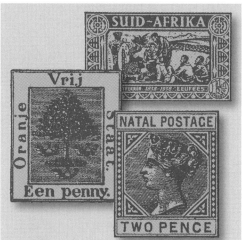

Legacy
Boers, fleeing British control, entered the territories of indigenous peoples. These 19th-century stamps record the creation of three Boer republics: Orange Free State; South African Republic and Natalia (later known as Transvaal and Natal respectively).

The British arrive at the Cape
A combination of English and Scottish settlers arrive in 1820 at Algoa Bay, near present-day Port Elizabeth.

During the 18th century, a wealthy elite developed in and around Cape Town and tensions developed between the Cape authorities and the Boers.

In that time many Boers began to move inland away from what they saw as the oppressive Dutch administration. Arriving in the Karoo region, they developed huge cattle farms. As pastures became exhausted, they moved on to more fertile areas. Known as *trekboers*, from the Dutch "*trek*," meaning to pull a wagon, these frontier farming people were strict Calvinists. They developed a powerful Afrikaner identity, seeing themselves as a distinct cultural and God-chosen group, which considered itself superior to the indigenous peoples. Away from the powerful influence of the Company the Boers became accustomed to making their own decisions and to dealing with Africans as they wished, often with great ferocity.

Having crossed the mountains inland of Cape Town, the Boers expanded rapidly to the east and north, setting up new districts, such as Swellendam (1745) and Graaff-Reinet (1785). They reached the grasslands north of the Olifants River by the 1750s, and the Sunday River by the 1760s, where they encountered the Xhosa.

The Boers came into conflict with the Khoisan, whose cattle they raided. When the Khoisan retaliated, the Boers formed militia-style groups which they called *kommmandos*, who raided the Khoisan, seizing their cattle, plundering their lands, and taking prisoners. In 1775 the Boers began to "apprentice" Khoisan children, and by the end of the 18th century some Khoisan were subject to a pass system, which meant that they needed permission to move around the area.

British arrivals

In 1795 and 1799 the Boers rebelled against the Cape authorities, arguing that the Company had not given them military protection against the Africans, nor recognized their land claims.

The rebellions were unsuccessful but by this time the British had also arrived at the Cape. In 1795 the British occupied Cape Colony, and in 1806 took permanent control of Cape Town. In 1820, some 5,000 government-assisted British immigrants arrived to settle in the Cape. The British immediately introduced changes, particularly to land ownership, which angered the Boers.

In 1807 Britain ended the slave trade, introduced passes and employment codes for Africans, and in 1833 abolished slavery in British colonies. The British also emphasized that Africans were to be treated as equals to whites, although in practice this did not happen.

Boer migrations

Unwilling to remain under British control, several thousand Afrikaners left the Cape, traveling north and east inland in a series of mass migrations. Now known collectively as the Great Trek, the journeys figure prominently in Afrikaner history.

The migrating Boers, who were known as *voortrekkers*, wanted their independence, particularly from British regulations. They also knew that vast areas north and east of them had been disrupted or depopulated by a series of African wars and migrations, which took place in the 1820s, known as the *Mfecane* (or *Difaqane*).

Travelling in huge family groups, the Afrikaners crossed the Drakensberg mountains, and then entered the territory of indigenous Bantu-speaking Africans. They encountered the Zulu and, after defeating them, set up a republic, Natalia, in 1839. Its capital was Pietermaritzburg. The Boers made Port Natal, now Durban, part of the republic, but in 1842 the British annexed the port and in 1843, annexed Natalia, which later became known as Natal.

The Boers then trekked back over the mountains where they founded more republics. In 1854, they founded the Orange Free State, which had previously been home to Bantu-speaking peoples, such as the Tswana and Sotho. They also founded the South African Republic (later known as Transvaal) out of several independent republics in the Highveld region.

Adam Kok III and the Griqua
The Griqua were mixed-race people of Afrikaner and African origin. Heavily Europeanized, they were Christians, dressed in European clothes, and spoke Dutch but were completely rejected by Boer society.

In the late 1700s, some began migrating northwards, setting up their own territory, called Griqualand, near the junction of the Orange and Vaal Rivers. From the 1820s, migrating Boers began settling on and buying their land.

In 1860, Griqua leader, Adam Kok III, led about 2,000 Griqua out of the territory, which became known as Griqualand West, on an eastward trek that lasted two years. Migrating through what is now Lesotho, they finally settled in a fertile area on the Drakensberg slopes, where they founded Griqualand East. In 1871, the British annexed Griqualand West; eight years later, Griqualand East became part of Cape Colony.

© DIAGRAM

Conflicts with Africans

In the mid-17th century, when the Dutch began settling what is now South Africa, indigenous kingdoms already existed over much of Southern Africa. As the Dutch laid down their colonial roots, they soon came into conflict with Africans.

Dutch-Khoikhoi Wars

At first the Dutch settlers traded with the Khoikhoi for cattle but as their demands increased, the Khoikoi began to put up resistance. Company officials turned to force, seizing Khoikhoi chiefs on charges of crimes and demanding cattle as ransom. Resistance grew and two major wars took place during the 17th century. In 1657 Khoikhoi clans, who had been cut off from their summer pastures and the fresh water of the Cape peninsula, attacked the Dutch settlement and beseiged it for nearly a year. Under the terms of the peace treaty, the Khoikhoi were forced to accept that the Dutch were entitled to buy their land; in practice the settlers seized any land and cattle they wanted.

A second conflict occurred in 1673–1677 when the company raided the Cochoqua people in the north, whom they accused of attacking white traders and hunters. They seized large numbers of cattle.

Khoisan resistance

During the 18th century, as the trekboers expanded rapidly to the north and east, they seized Khoisan grazing lands and cattle. Cattle raids and counter raids were a continuous fact of life throughout the century as either the Khoisan attacked Boer farms and seized their cattle, or Boer kommando groups raided the Khoisan, plundering cattle, seizing their lands, and forcing dispossessed Khoisan into laboring as servants or farm workers.

By the final years of the 18th century, the colony's northern frontier was under arms and many Dutch settlers had been driven off. Between 1799 and 1803, dispossessed Khoisan farm workers in the Graaff-Reinet region, many armed with horses and guns, rebelled against the colonists. Government troops intervened to put down the rebellion – the last attempt by the Khoisan to save their lost lands.

Cape-Xhosa Wars

Conflict also occurred on the eastern frontier during the 1770s when trekboers moving east clashed with the Xhosa, one of the main groups who had emerged from the Nguni people. Xhoso clans had established chiefdoms along the eastern coast, from

A cattle raid
As the Boers expanded their territory they encountered the Khoisan. This illustration portrays a Boer kommando group raiding a Khoisan settlement.

the Sunday and Kei rivers, inland to the Drakensberg Mountains.

Initially, the Xhosa traded with the Dutch but, as the colonial settlements expanded, relations deteriorated and violence broke out in a series of nine frontier wars which lasted on and off for about 100 years.

The first Cape-Xhosa Wars lasted from 1779–1781. War was sparked off when a small party of Boers crossed the Fish River, killing a Xhosa herdsman and seizing cattle. The Xhosa reacted fiercely, seizing thousands of cattle until forced back by Boer kommandos. Over the next few years, war dragged on in a series of raids and counter raids. Using guerrilla tactics, the Xhosa hid in forests, emerging at night to recapture their cattle, or raided isolated farms while Boer kommandos were not gathered in the vicinity.

War began again in 1793 when Boers attacked Xhosa who had crossed the Fish River. The Xhosa

Xhosa warrior
During the 1770s the Boers began to encroach onto Xhosa territory, and a series of wars followed which lasted until the next century.

put up a fierce resistance, capturing thousands of cattle and destroying many farms. The Xhosa were victorious and the Boers were forced to make peace. A third war took place between 1799–1803 when war with the Xhosa coincided with an uprising of Khoisan servants. The British, who then controlled the Cape, managed to divide the African forces by making some concessions to the Khoisan, but were unable to move the Xhosa, who were entrenched in an area west of the Great Fish River. Xhosa fighters defeated a large Boer kommando force and remained victorious.

The Boers never managed to defeat the Xhosa but, from 1811, British troops arrived on the Cape frontier. Throughout the 19th century, British forces continued to fight the Xhosa, who fought heroically but were defeated at the end of the century. The Cape authorities took over their last independent kingdom in 1895.

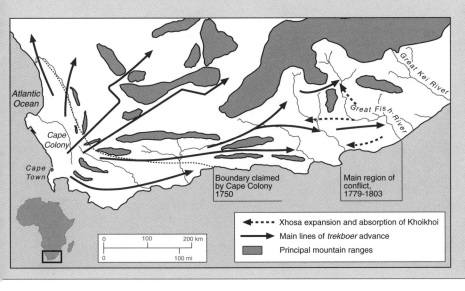

Atlantic Ocean

Cape Colony

Cape Town

Great Kei River

Great Fish River

Boundary claimed by Cape Colony 1750

Main region of conflict, 1779-1803

Xhosa expansion and absorption of Khoikhoi

Main lines of *trekboer* advance

Principal mountain ranges

0   100   200 km
0   100 mi

Moving towards conflict
This map shows the eastward expansion of the Boer settlements during the period 1660–1800, and also the main region of conflict with the Xhosa, 1779–1803.

© DIAGRAM

The Great Trek

In search of new pastures
Afrikaner farmers, Khoikhoi and their herds of sheep and cattle, travel inland from the Cape.

Between 1835 and 1837 more than 7,000 Boers – men, women, and children – left Cape Colony on a series of mass migrations north and east that later became known as the Great Trek. Their journeying did not end until 1848. During their travels, they encountered and fought the Zulu and Ndebele.

Voortrekkers

The Boer migrants who took part in the Great Trek were known as voortrekkers, and their exploits and the Trek itself have become an integral part of Afrikaner history and legend. They left the Cape to escape British control and new legislation that the British were introducing, which appeared to favor Africans, and to find new, independent lands where they could establish their own territory built on their belief in themselves as God's chosen people.

The voortrekkers, who were accompanied by some 7,000 servants, traveled in huge family groups. They sold or abandoned their farms, and packed all their possessions, including household utensils, supplies and Bibles, into massive ox-drawn wagons, some 12 feet in length. The wheels of the wagons were as high as a man's shoulder. They also brought with them their cattle, sheep, and goats. They survived on meat and milk from their livestock, by hunting and sometimes by trading with local African farmers. Travel was slow and the voortrekkers covered only a few miles every day.

The first groups set out in 1835 under the leadership of Louis Trichardt and Hans van Rensburg. Other groups, under the command of the leaders Andries Pretorius, Gert Maritz, and Piet Retief followed. A huge Boer camp of several thousand voortrekkers eventually gathered in the region of what we know today as the Orange Free State. The voortrekkers then headed for what is now Natal, in an effort to find land suitable for grazing and settlement.

Conflict

During their migrations, the voortrekkers *met fierce resistance from Africans, such as the Zulu and Ndebele. Their battles and victories are still celebrated by Afrikaners as proof that God supports their cause. In 1836, a large group of* voortrekkers, *led by Hendrik Potgieter, arrived on the southern Highveld and clashed with the Ndebele at the Battle of Vegkop. They were rescued by the Rolong, who were themselves warring with the Ndebele. Following their victory, Potgieter claimed the whole of the former Ndebele kingdom.*

In 1837, voortrekkers *traveling east over the Drakensberg Mountains came into conflict with the Zulu, who lured their leaders into an ambush and attacked a* voortrekkers *camp at the foot of the mountains. However, in 1838, some 500* voortrekkers, *armed with superior gun power, defeated more than 3,000 Zulus at the Battle of Blood River, a victory that the Afrikaners claimed was a result of a divine pact with God. The victory enabled the Boers to found their first short-lived Boer republic of Natalia (now Natal).*

Boer republics

By 1848, the Great Trek was over. The Boers had established three republics: Natalia, the South African Republic (later Transvaal), and the Orange Free State. Britain annexed all the republics, but subsequently recognized the Transvaal and Orange Free State as independent Boer republics. The Trek also profoundly disrupted African kingdoms on the Highveld and in the southeastern interior, particularly the Ndebele and Zulu. The Zulu recovered but the Ndebele were forced to rebuild their kingdom farther north.

Voice of a nation
In 1837 Piet Retief, an Afrikaner of French Huguenot descent, published a manifesto outlining the reasons why the Boers felt the need to undertake The Great Trek.

The Battle of Vegkop, 1836
Voortrekkers from the eastern Cape clashed with the Ndebele at Vegkop; the Boers defended their position successfully, with the result that the Ndebele were expelled from the Transvaal highveld in 1837.

© DIAGRAM

THE *MFECANE* (CRUSHING)

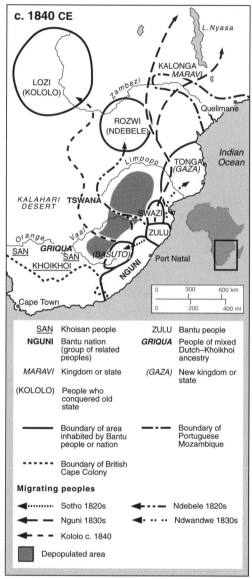

c. 1840 CE

L.Nyasa

KALONGA
MARAVI

LOZI
(KOLOLO)

Zambezi

Quelimane

ROZWI
(NDEBELE)

Indian
Ocean

Limpopo

TONGA
(GAZA)

KALAHARI
DESERT   TSWANA

SWAZI

Orange   Vaal   ZULU

SAN   GRIQUA   (BASUTO)
KHOIKHOI   SAN   Port Natal

NGUNI

Cape Town

| 0 | 300 | 600 km |
| 0 | 200 | 400 mi |

SAN	Khoisan people	ZULU	Bantu people
NGUNI	Bantu nation (group of related peoples)	*GRIQUA*	People of mixed Dutch–Khoikhoi ancestry
MARAVI	Kingdom or state	(GAZA)	New kingdom or state
(KOLOLO)	People who conquered old state		

Boundary of area inhabited by Bantu people or nation — Boundary of Portuguese Mozambique

Boundary of British Cape Colony

Migrating peoples

Sotho 1820s — Ndebele 1820s

Nguni 1830s — Ndwandwe 1830s

Kololo c. 1840

Depopulated area

The *Mfecane* (Crushing)
After the Zulu expansion of 1817, Southern Africa entered a period known as the *Mfecane*. Shaka, the Zulu leader, launched a series of such ferocious attacks on neighboring peoples that mass migrations followed. Many people fled north or south, some forming new states, others displacing existing ones. Zulu power waned with the death of Shaka in 1828, by which time the death toll had risen to 2 million.

Between about 1819–1839, a series of mass migrations and wars between African states occurred in the eastern half of Southern Africa, largely as an effect of the rise of the Zulu nation. The Nguni call the events *Mfecane*, or the Crushing; the Sotho-Tswana, who lived west of the Drakensberg, call them *Difaqane*, or the scattering.

The events sent shock waves through the region, and farther afield, as millions of Africans died or became refugees, and populations and chiefdoms were forced to move to new territories. From the disruption emerged new states, including the Swazi, Sotho, and Matebele kingdoms. The latter stages of the *Mfecane* coincided with the Boers' Great Trek, and were some of the reasons why not only the Boers but also other Europeans were able to penetrate the area relatively easily.

Early conflicts

By the early 19th century, there were several Nguni chiefdoms in the coastal regions east of the Drakensberg Mountains. Three of the most powerful were situated in what is now the South African province known as KwaZulu/Natal and the southern part of Swaziland. They were the Ndwandwe, who had created a powerful and centralized state under their leader Zwide, the Ngwane under Sobhuza, and the Mthethwa, led by Dingiswayo. Others included the Ngwane, Khumalo, and Zulu.

The latter half of the 18th century had been peaceful but following a long period of drought in which pastures dried up and cattle died, the Ndwandwe began attacking their neighbors and raiding their cattle. In 1816 Zwide launched an attack on the Ngwane, forcing them north of the Pongola River into what is now Swaziland. Some historians argue that this event triggered the *Mfecane*, while others believe it began a little later.

Zwide's armies went on to defeat the Mthethwa kingdom. Dingiswayo was killed in battle, his regiments were scattered and his kingdom destroyed, leaving the Ndwandwe supreme in the region. However, they were soon superseded by the Zulus.

Zulu expansion

In 1816 Shaka, a Zulu and one of Dingiswayo's generals, had seized the throne to become leader of the Zulu chiefdom. A brilliant general, he turned his regiments into a powerful fighting force and from 1817 began a series of ferocious attacks against neighboring chiefdoms, probably to gain cattle and more grazing lands.

In 1818, following Dingiswayo's defeat, Shaka brought the shattered Mthethwa kingdom under his control. Determined to defeat the new threat, Zwide attacked Shaka, who withdrew his entire people, leaving the land bare of livestock and crops. When the Ndwandwe turned back, Shaka launched a successful attack. Zwide escaped and a flood of Ndwandwe refugees fled north of the Pongola River. Two of Zwide 's generals – Soshangane and Zwangendabe – led what remained of the army north of Delagoa Bay.

Shaka now controlled a vast region from the Pongola River to the Tugela. He continued to expand his empire, attacking one chiefdom after another in the region east of the Drakensberg Mountains. Thousands were killed and much of what is now present-day Natal was all but deserted. Some survivors were absorbed into the expanding Zulu nation, while others became refugees who fled, or were driven north and south in successive waves. Some fleeing south sought safety with the Mpondo and Thembu. One group of refugees reached the Xhosa, who named them *mfengu*, meaning beggars. Later the same refugees made alliances with the British to fight the Xhosa.

Shaka (left)
He founded the Zulu kingdom in 1818, but was later murdered by his half-brothers in 1828.

A Zulu hatchet (right)
Many had brass wire wound around the wooden shaft which made them formidable weapons.

Zulu warriors (right)
During the period known as the *Mfecane*, Zulu warriors formed the spearhead of the attacks led by Shaka on neighboring peoples.

©DIAGRAM

New kingdoms: Swazi and Gaza state

Rival chiefdoms

Ferocious attacks between neighboring chiefdoms were often undertaken to gain more cattle and richer grazing land. Survivors were absorbed into the expanding Zulu nation, or became refugees, driven north and south in successive waves, who joined up with other chiefdoms, such as the Mpondo and Thembu.

Family at war

In 1828 after he and his brother Mhlangane assassinated their half-brother, Shaka, Dingane killed Mhlangane and then proclaimed himself king of the Zulu. Dingane is shown here in a restful pose with his dog.

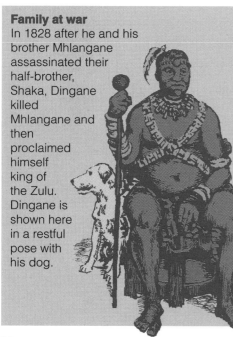

As the Nguni were driven over the Drakensberg Mountains by Shaka's armies, they encountered, raided, and fought with the groups that they found, creating a knock-on effect that spread the effects of the *Mfecane* further afield. West of the Drakensberg were the southern Sotho, and the Tswana, most of whom were organized in small independent kingdoms, and unprepared for the waves of desperate invaders. Events west of the Drakensberg are often called the *Difaqane*.

In 1821–1822 the Nguni, the Hlubi, then the Tlokwa, and Ngwane invaded the region, fleeing from the Zulu. Their arrival sparked off a cycle of warfare and destruction that spread across the Highveld. Crops and villages were burnt, thousands of people were killed in battle or through starvation and chiefdoms were disrupted, and destroyed or, in their turn, attacked others. One group that launched a series of attacks was known as Mantatees, and was led by a woman, MaNtatisi.

The latter stages of the *Mfecane*

Shaka was assassinated in 1828, and his brother Dingane seized control of the Zulu nation. He promised peace, but attacks, raids, and warfare continued for some years. They did not really die out until the late 1830s, when the Zulu began to come into contact with the growing numbers of white settlers.

Out of this turmoil came a number of new kingdoms, including the Swazi nation, the Basotho kingdom, the Ndebele, and the Gaza state. Many were forerunners of today's Southern African nations.

Swazi kingdom

The Swazi, who were a northern Nguni kingdom in Natal when the *Mfecane* began, were forced to move north-westward. After Zwide's Ndwandwe had driven the Ngwane northward, the Ngwane, led by Sobhuza, retreated to the mountains around the upper Nkomati River. In 1819 Sobhuza led the Ngwane back southward to the Usuthu valley and began to create a new nation. A number of Sotho, also fleeing from the Zulu, were absorbed into the new kingdom. To avoid conflict, Sobhuza paid tribute to the Zulu kings, but nevertheless was raided by the Zulu on many occasions. He held his own but in 1839 Sobhuza died during a raid and was succeeded by his son and heir, Mswati, who was only 13, so his mother Thandile ruled in his stead. Thandile centralized the kingdom, setting up regiments and royal villages. When Mswati became ruler, he named the new nation Swazi after himself. Mswati's reign ended in 1865, by which time the Swazi kingdom was powerful.

Gaza state

Following their defeat in 1819, Zwide's Ndwandwe state fell apart and refugees from the state fled northwards, moving into southern Mozambique. There they re-organized themselves around former rulers and became known as the Ngoni. By the 1830s, Soshangane was their most important leader. Over the years, he created a powerful military state, raiding an area that extended from Delagoa Bay to the Zambezi valley. He named the state Gaza, after his grandfather. The state grew rich by raiding and exacting tribute. The original Ndwandwe were the ruling class and military elite, calling themselves Ngoni. Ordinary people were called Shangaan.

Shangane warrior
This illustration, based on an early 20th-century photograph, shows a warrior, old at the time, dressed in traditional Shangane costume.

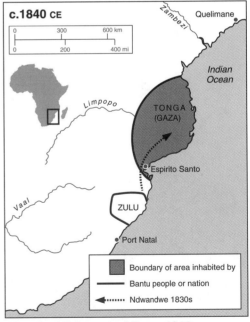

c.1840 CE

Boundary of area inhabited by
Bantu people or nation
Ndwandwe 1830s

The establishment of Gaza, 1840
Refugees from the Ndwandwe kingdom fled into an area, known then as the Gaza state, and which is now southern Mozambique.

57

New kingdoms: Basotho, Kololo, Matabele and Shona

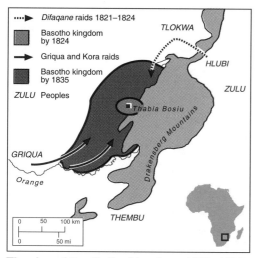

The rise of the Sotho kingdom, 1830–1835
By 1831 the Sotho defeated the invading army of the Ndebele, and soon became the most powerful nation on the Highveld.

In about 1818 the Sotho chief Moshoeshoe I led a coalition of Sotho people to safety in what is now Lesotho. Attacked by Nguni groups, and disrupted by the *Mfecane*, the Sotho created a secure stronghold on a flat-topped mountain (Thaba-Bosiu) to provide a refuge. From the 1820s, Moshoeshoe offered protection to various refugees; by 1824 Moshoeshoe had some 21,000 followers, with whom he created an entirely new nation, the Basotho kingdom, the forerunner of modern Lesotho. In 1831 the Sotho defeated invading Ndebele and when the *Mfecane* ended, the Sotho kingdom was the most powerful nation on the Highveld.

Kololo

Another new group that emerged in the Highveld was the Kololo, which consisted of fragmented groups of Sotho people. They attacked and disrupted existing Tswana groups in what is now Botstwana. Attacks by invading Ndebele forced the Kololo to move north. Under the leadership of Sebetwane, they eventually arrived in the lands of the Lozi and settled on the upper Zambezi in the 1840s.

Sotho weapons (right)
During the period 1818–1831 the Sotho were engaged in a series of conflicts with other chiefdoms. Their supremacy in battle owed much to the precision and skill with which their weapons were made.

Moshoeshoe (1786–1870) (left)
A Sotho chief who created the kingdom of Basotho (now Lesotho), he united the clans of the Sotho people, fought off attacks by neighboring chiefdoms, and later fought the British and the Boers.

Matabele kingdom

The Matabele also emerged in the 19th century. Their leader Mzilikazi was Shaka's lieutenant and one of the Khumalo, a Ndebele group that had not migrated north. In 1823, Mzilikazi broke from Shaka and led the Khumalo to settle north of the Vaal River. There he began to set up a powerful Ndebele kingdom near what is now Tshwane (Pretoria). Repeatedly attacked by Zulu, Griqua, Kora, and Boers, Mzilikazi led his people to a new settlement, which he called Bulawayo (The Place of Slaughter), in what is now Zimbabwe. He created another Ndebele kingdom, which became known as Matabele.

Shona kingdoms

By the time of the *Mfecane*, the Rozvi Empire of the Shona people had collapsed. In its place were more than 100 small Shona states. These too were disrupted by Shaka's expansion, when the Matabele began to arrive in what is now southern Zimbabwe. Matabele arrivals gave the many groups the name Shona.

Mzilikazi (1790–1868)
He was the founder of the Ndebele (Matabele) kingdom located around Bulawayo. This kingdom later became known as Matabeleland, and is now Zimbabwe. Mzilikazi led the Ndebele northward from Natal to Transvaal to escape from the Zulu under Dingane, and even farther north to escape from the Boer settlers.

The *Mfecane* (Crushing)

1806	British take Cape Colony from Dutch
1815	Nguni kingdoms Ndwandwe, Ngwane, and Mthethwa dominate Natal region
1818–1819	Zulu-Ndwandwe war: Zulus establish supremacy in Natal region
1818–1828	Shaka creates powerful Zulu kingdom
c. 1818	Chief Moshoeshoe leads coalition of people into Lesotho region to escape Shaka
1819–1839	*Mfecane* (or *Difaqane*): period of mass migrations and wars
1820s	Mzilikazi founds Ndebele kingdom
1824	Moshoeshoe founds Basotho kingdom
1830s	Gaza state (Ngoni) emerges in what is now Mozambique
1830s	Migrating Kololo and Ndebele peoples attack Tswana, Botswana
1831	Sotho defeat Ndebele who invade their territory
1835–1848	Boers make Great Trek
1836–1837	Boers battle with Ndebele who migrate north to present-day Zimbabwe
1838	Battle of Blood River: Boers defeat Zulu
1839	Natalia (Boer republic) created
1843	British seize Natalia, which becomes British colony called Natal
1839–1865	Mswati I reigns over Ngwane; creates Swazi nation
1851–1852	Sotho-British wars
1856–1868	Boers try to conquer Basotho
1860–1867	Venda and Sotho drive Boers from lands north of Olifants River
1869	Basotho becomes British colony called Basutoland

Defense
A Zulu shield made from wood and animal skin.

© DIAGRAM

Zulu warriors

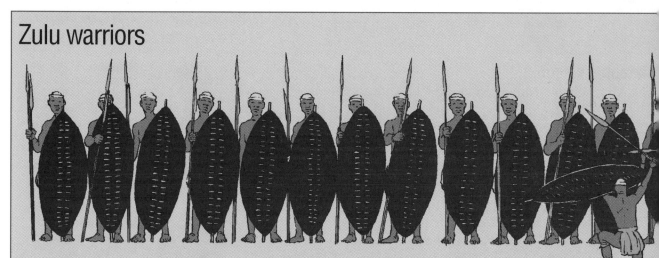

In 1816 Shaka seized the throne to become king of the Zulu. Within a few years, he turned a minor Zulu clan into a mighty empire. As leader, he introduced a number of military changes to create the most highly trained and disciplined fighting force that had ever been seen in the region.

Warfare transformed

Traditionally when the Nguni went to war they relied on raiding cattle from their enemies, and on displaying a show of strength. Two opposing armies hurled spears at each other until one side retreated. The victorious army then seized large numbers of cattle from the defeated people. Casualties were low. Shaka transformed warfare in the region by developing a strategy of total warfare that would completely devastate his enemies and prevent them from recovering. He wiped out armies, killed opponents, including women and children, and destroyed homesteads as well as seizing cattle. To do this he introduced severe military discipline and innovatory fighting techniques, which turned his warriors into a well-drilled fighting machine.

Some of the fighting techniques that Shaka introduced had already been used by other groups, but what Shaka did was to combine the techniques, improve them, and make them into a highly effective, cohesive military strategy.

Age-regiments

Zulu warriors were organized into permanent age-regiments, men of a particular age group who were called on to work or fight for a chief. Previously, age-regiments had been temporary arrangements. After initiation into adulthood, young men served their chiefs for a limited period until being released for marriage. Shaka ended initiation ceremonies, and organized all young men into age-regiments for long or semi-permanent periods. Men were forbidden to marry before the age of 40, and regiments could only be disbanded and men released for marriage when they had achieved distinction in battle or were too old for fighting.

The Zulu nation in its prime	
300s–400s	Bantu-speaking peoples reach what is now Natal
1787	Shaka born
1816	Shaka becomes leader of the Zulu
1818–1819	War between Zulu and Ndwandwe: Zulu achieve supremacy
1819–1839	Mfecane (and Difaqane): Wars and mass migrations in eastern Southern Africa
1828	Shaka assassinated by his half-brothers, Dingane and Mhlangane. Dingane succeeds Shaka as leader
1838	Battle of Blood River: Boers defeat Zulu
1840	Mpande becomes Zulu leader
1872	Cetshwayo becomes Zulu king
1879	British conquer Zulu

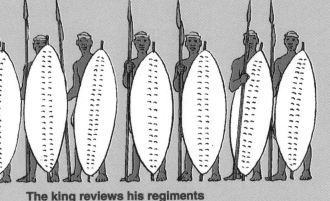

The king reviews his regiments

This illustration shows King Panda (with arm raised) inspecting two regiments, each with different colored shields. Zulu warriors were singled out from regiments and ordered to demonstrate their athletic prowess.

Training, tactics, and weapons

Discipline was severe and warriors had to undergo strenuous training. They were taken from their homesteads and had to live in military camps around the empire. They had to discard their leather sandals to toughen their feet, and learned to run and fight barefoot, jogging from battle to battle and sprinting into the fight. Warriors were armed with short stabbing spears, for close combat, and carried long shields for protection, which could be locked together to form a tortoise-shell style barrier. Punishments were severe: any Zulu warrior accused of cowardice was executed.

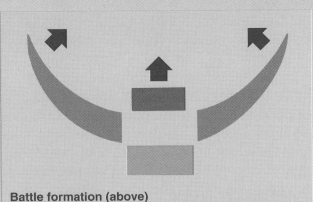

Battle formation (above)

Shaka also made use of a new battle formation, sometimes called the "cow horn," which may have been used by others before him. In this tactic, the main part of the Zulu army (the chest) faced the enemy, while regiments (the horns) were sent out on each side. The main part charged ahead, and the regiments prevented the opposing force from escaping.

Zulu peoples today (above)

This map shows the modern extent of the Zulu peoples in Southern Africa, together with their former homelands.

© DIAGRAM

Madagascar is the world's fourth largest island. It is situated in the Indian Ocean about 250 miles (400km) off the coast of Mozambique. Its people consist of two main groups: those of Indonesian descent, who live mainly on the highlands in the center of the island, and those of African origin, who live on the coastal region.

Early history

Madagascar's early history is unclear but the first people to arrive were probably Malayo-Polynesian seafarers who settled on Madagascar about 2,000 to 1,500 years ago. They may have come, in successive waves, via the African coast.

From about the 900s Muslim traders coming from eastern Africa and the Comoros set up trading colonies in the north of the island where, from the 14th century, they introduced Islam. In the 11th century, Bantu-speaking Africans also began to arrive on the island of Madagascar.

Powerful kingdoms

From the 1400s a number of small kingdoms emerged on Madagascar, including those of the Antemoro, Antaisaka, Bétsiléo, and Merina. Three powerful kingdoms emerged, which were formed by the unification of the smaller states. In the late 1500s, the Sakalava kingdom, under Andriandahifotsi, emerged on the west coast and conquered west and north Madagascar.

By the mid-1700s it controlled nearly half of the island but the kingdom disintegrated after the death of its last ruler, Queen Ravahiny in 1808.

In the 17th century, an alliance of chiefdoms, called the Tsitambala Conference, sprang up on the east coast. The confederation was taken over and expanded by Ratsimilaho, the son of an English pirate, who created the Betsimisaraka kingdom.

Sculpture or ritual?
The top half of a wooden post, dating from the 19thcentury, that may have been used as a tomb sculpture by the Mahafaly, or as a village ritual post by the Sakalava. It has also been attributed to many other Madagascan peoples from time to time.

An ancestral tomb
Often the focus of festivals and ceremonies, ancestral tombs signify a person's place in society and their rights to land. This particular tomb, belonging to a noble house, consists of a burial vault on the bottom, and a prayer house on the top.

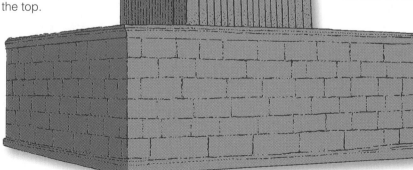

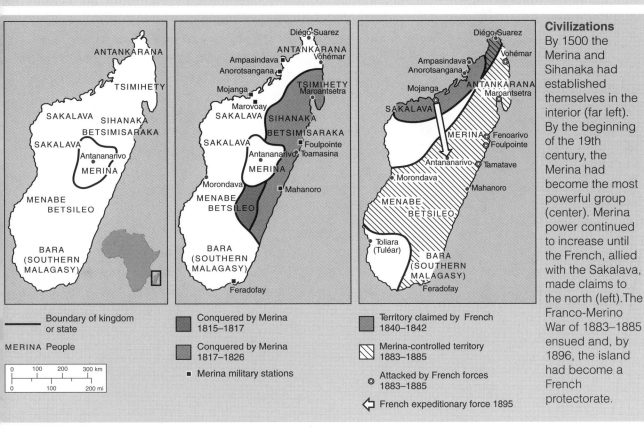

Boundary of kingdom or state

MERINA People

| 0 | 100 | 200 | 300 km |
| 0 | 100 | | 200 mi |

■ Conquered by Merina 1815–1817

■ Conquered by Merina 1817–1826

■ Merina military stations

■ Territory claimed by French 1840–1842

▨ Merina-controlled territory 1883–1885

◎ Attacked by French forces 1883–1885

◁ French expeditionary force 1895

Civilizations

By 1500 the Merina and Sihanaka had established themselves in the interior (far left). By the beginning of the 19th century, the Merina had become the most powerful group (center). Merina power continued to increase until the French, allied with the Sakalava, made claims to the north (left).The Franco-Merino War of 1883–1885 ensued and, by 1896, the island had become a French protectorate.

However, the one that was to be the most powerful was the Merina kingdom, which emerged in the central highlands during the 1400s, when the Merina settled there and conquered the original inhabitants, the Vazimba.

At the end of the 1700s, the Merina people were united under King Andrianampoinimerina (reigned 1787–1810) who also subjugated the Bétsiléo. In 1791 the Betsimisaraka kingdom collapsed, followed by the Sakalava kingdom in 1822.

In the early 19th century, the Merina, under their ruler Radama I (reigned 1810–1828) and with British assistance, systematically took over much of the island. In exchange for agreeing to end the slave trade, Radama I received British aid to modernize and equip his army, which allowed him to subdue Betsimisaraka kingdom.

Andrianampoin-imerina

A Merina king, he created a unified state in Madagascar by 1797.

King Radama I

The son and successor of Andrianampoin-imerina, he extended Merina control over most of Madagascar.

© DIAGRAM

European arrivals in Madagascar

Vasco da Gama
A Portuguese explorer, in 1497–1499 he sailed down the coast of West Africa, around the Cape of Good Hope, via Madagascar, to Sri Lanka, and then India. His intention was to open up routes to the East, and set up trading posts along the way.

Shipwrecked on the rocks
During the late 17th and early 18th centuries, many European pirates used Madagascar as a base from which to raid merchant shipping in the Indian Ocean.

The first European to see the island was Portuguese navigator Diogo Dias in 1500. More Portuguese ships arrived, which raided the Muslim settlements and, in the early 1600s, Portuguese Roman Catholic missionaries tried unsuccessfully to convert the Malagasy. The British, French, and Dutch also arrived in Madagascar. From 1643 until the late 1700s, the French established footholds at Taolonaro (Fort Dauphin) in the southeast, and on Sainte Marie Island off the east coast, but all European attempts to establish colonies were repeatedly destroyed by the islanders.

Relations with Europe
In the early 1800s, Radama I, king of the Merina, opened the island to foreigners, particularly the French and British. He welcomed British and French missionaries to the island, including the Protestant London Missionary Society, which gained many converts, opened schools,

and helped to transcribe the Merina language. In 1817 the British acknowledged Radama I as king of Madagascar.

Radama I died in 1828 and was succeeded by his wife Ranavalona I (reigned 1828–1861) who was far more suspicious of foreigners and reversed his policies. In 1835 she declared Christianity illegal, halted most foreign trade, closed down the schools and churches, and expelled many European missionaries and traders. During her rule, civil war wracked the Merina.

In 1861, after Ranavalona's death, the French and British began to return to Madagascar. Under Radama II (reigned 1861–1863), and his widow and successor, Rasoherina (reigned 1863–1868), the anti-European policy was reversed once more, and missionaries and European traders were welcomed back.

Rainilaiarivony, the prime minister, controlled the government during the reigns of Ranavalona II (1868–1883), and Ranavalona III (1883–1897). By 1885 the Merina kingdom included all of Madagascar except the south and part of the west.

Rainilaiarivony
He was prime minister of Madagascar from 1864–1896, and controlled the government during the reigns of the last two Queen Ranavalonas.

Ranavalona I
This illustration is adapted from one which appeared in an issue of *The Illustrated London News*, dated 1845. The Queen of Madagascar is shown in a regal pose, carried aloft by her attendants in a *howdah*, or seat, and surrounded by her faithful subjects.

©DIAGRAM

The Franco-Merina Wars

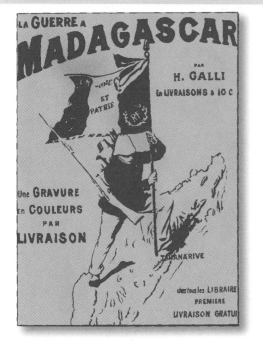

Victory for France
This poster graphically portrays the defeat of Madagascar at the hands of the French in the Second Franco-Merina War which started in 1895.

From 1861, France, Britain, and the Merina quarreled over control of the island and between 1883–1885 France and the Merina went to war. In 1883 the French bombarded and occupied Tamatave (now Toamasina) and in 1885 established a protectorate over the island. In 1890 Britain agreed to let France have Madagascar in exchange for British control of Egypt and Zanzibar.

Five years later Madagascar was declared a French protectorate. The Merina refused to submit and war broke out again in 1895 when prime minister Rainilaiarivony organized resistance to the French. Heavy fighting continued until 1896 but the French imposed their rule by force. French troops under J.S. Gallieni landed on the northwest coast and occupied Antananarivo.

A further rebellion, known as *menelamba*, broke out in 1896 but was suppressed with great brutality. Queen Ranavalona III was forced to recognize the French protectorate, and allowed to remain on the throne as a figurehead. The monarchy was abolished in 1897 and she was deposed.

End of an era
This vivid illustration, based on a journal of the time, depicts Queen Ranavalona III being deposed from her position as Queen of Madagascar. The Second Franco-Merina War, which started in 1895, resulted in Madagascar being declared a French colony. Although Ranavalona III was allowed to remain on the throne, she was eventually deposed and the monarchy abolished in 1897.

General J. S. Gallieni
General Gallieni was in control of the French forces in the Second Franco-Merina War in 1895. He became Governor-General following the suppression of the *menelamba* rebellion in November 1896.

Colonialism and independence

By 1904 France was in full control of Madagascar but Merina nationalism and resistance to the French soon developed. In 1916 the French suppressed a Merina secret society that was plotting against the colonists.

During World War II (1939–1945), Madagascar aligned itself with Vichy France until 1942 when the British conquered the island. In 1943, the Free French took control. From 1947–1948 there was a major uprising against the French which was brutally suppressed.

Merina nationalist activity increased during the 1950s and the Social Democratic Party (PSD), headed by Philibert Tsiranana, gained prominence. In 1958 the Malagasy people agreed to become self-governing within the French Community. In 1959 Tsiranana was elected president. In 1960 Madagascar finally became a fully independent country.

Philibert Tsiranana
He became first president of a newly-named, independent, Malagasy Republic in 1960.

Madagascar: from settlement to independence	
100s–400s CE	Indonesian peoples settle Madagascar
900s–1200s	Muslims from East Africa settle northern Madagascar
1500	Portuguese navigator Diogo Dias is the first European to visit Madagascar
1506–1507	Portuguese destroy Muslim trading towns
1600s	Merina kingdom founded
1643	French establish Fort Dauphin, southern Madagascar; they abandon it in 1671
1680–1720	Pirates use the island as a base
1700s	Sakalava kingdom dominant
1787–1810	Merina win control of most of Madagascar
1810	King Radama I outlaws slave trade
1817	Britain recognizes Radama I as king
1845	Radama's widow, Queen Ranavalona I, defeats Anglo-French invasion and expels Europeans
1861	King Radama II grants concessions to French traders
1883–1885	First Franco-Merina War
1890	Madagascar becomes French protectorate
1895	Second Franco-Merina War
1896	Madagascar declared a French colony
1897	Queen Ranavalona III deposed, last monarch
1920	France suppresses nationalist movement
1939–1945	World War II: British and South African forces occupy Madagascar, which is handed over to Free French
1947	Pro-independence rebellion begins
1948	France suppresses rebellion; 80,000 killed
1950–1959	Internal self-government
1960	Independence achieved

POSTAGE.
BRITISH VICE-CONSULATE
ANTANANARIVO
ONE PENNY.

Consular mail
In March 1884 the British Vice-Consul issued stamps for use on both local and overseas mail.

© DIAGRAM

67

MAURITIUS

Prince John Maurice of Nassau-Siegen
He was the head of state in Holland when a Dutch squadron landed at Grand Port in Mauritius in 1598; the island was named in his honor. The Dutch retained control of the island until they decided to leave in 1710.

A former resident
The dodo was a flightless pigeon, as big as a large turkey, which was hunted to extinction by the Dutch settlers on the island of Mauritius three centuries ago.

Mauritius lies east of Madagascar in the Indian Ocean. Originally uninhabited, it was visited by Arabs, and the Dutch, and settled by the French and British.

Early arrivals and settlements

Portuguese navigators reached what is now Mauritius in 1510 and found it uninhabited. Arab sailors may have visited Mauritius during the Middle Ages and, on maps dated about 1500, it is shown with an Arab name, *Dina Arobi*. The first European to land was probably the Portuguese sailor, Domingo Fernandez Pereira, but the Portuguese did not stay.

In 1598 a Dutch squadron landed at Grand Port and named the island Mauritius, after Fürst Johann Moritz von Nassau-Siegen, the Dutch head of state. From then until 1710, the Dutch took control of the island, making an initial attempt at settlement in 1638. It was from here that the Dutch explorer Tasman set out to explore the western part of Australia. Tasmania is named in his honor.

Dutch settlements were not successful and they left the island in 1710 having introduced sugar cane, domestic animals, and deer. They also encountered the flightless dodo, which was hunted to extinction.

French control

In 1710 France took possession of Mauritius, which was a valuable port of call on the route to India, and named it Île de France. In 1722 French colonists from Réunion settled on the island, and gradually developed the economy, using slave labor to grow various crops. They also built Port Louis as a naval base and ship-building center. Under the governship of Mahe de La Bourdonnais, numerous buildings were erected, some of which still stand today. The French East India Company administered the island until 1767, after which time it was administered by French government officials.

During the French Revolution (1789–1792), Mauritians set up their own government. During the Napoleonic Wars (1803–1815), the French used Mauritius as a base to attack British ships. Raids continued until 1810 when a British expedition captured the island.

British control

The British made a first, unsuccessful, attempt to capture Mauritius, but a second attempt succeeded, and the British landed in large numbers on the island, quickly overpowering the French. In 1810, France relinquished control to the British who reinstated the name Mauritius.

Under British control, rapid social and economic changes took place. In 1833 the British abolished slavery, and more than 75,000 slaves were freed. Sugar became the main crop and, between 1835–1907, the planters imported more than 450,000 indentured laborers from India. Most were Hindus, although some were Muslims. A small number of Chinese traders followed. The immigrants were often badly treated and immigration finally ended in 1913.

Independence

In 1825 the British set up a Council of Government. The Council was expanded in 1886 to allow for elected representatives. In 1948, the franchise (right to vote) was extended to all adults who could pass a simple literacy test. A Legislative Council replaced the Council of Government and general elections were held for the first time in 1948. In 1958 the island became internally self-governing, and fully independent in 1968.

Mauritius under foreign control	
1510	Portuguese reach uninhabited island of Mauritius
1598–	Dutch take control
1710	Dutch make unsuccessful attempts to colonize the island and hunt flightless dodo, which is exterminated
1715	France takes control and re-names island Île de France
1722	French colonists arrive. Using slaves, some of whom come from Madagascar, they develop a crop-based economy.
c.1790	French revolutionary government tries to abolish slavery. Islanders break away from France
1810	Britain occupies the island, renaming it Mauritius
1833	Britain abolishes slavery, freeing more than 75,000 slaves. Britain imports indentured laborers from India to work sugar crop
c.1958	Mauritius gains internal self-government
1968	Mauritius becomes independent

Toiling on the plantation
European settlers, such as the Dutch in Mauritius, introduced sugar cane to their colonial possessions to satisfy the demand for sugar in Europe. Indigenous people were forced to harvest the crop, usually under harsh and demanding physical conditions.

© DIAGRAM

COMOROS

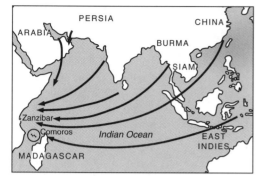

Indian Ocean trade, c.1500
This map shows the proximity of the Comoros islands to the African coast, and the importance of their position in relation to the trade routes from China, the East Indies, Southeast Asia, India and Arabia.

An Arabian *dhow*
Sailing boats, called *dhows*, used the monsoon winds to carry them across the water. Arabs, en route from a number of countries around the Indian Ocean, plied their trade along the eastern side of the African coastline, and the islands, like the Comoros, which were situated just off the coast.

Comoros is a small island country. It consists of a group of four islands in the Indian Ocean, situated between mainland Africa and northern Madagascar. Its population is ethnically mixed, reflecting the many differing peoples who arrived in the area.

Early history

Little is known about the first inhabitants of the Comoros, although archaeologists have found a settlement on Nzwani which dates back to the sixth century. According to legend, a Persian (Iranian) king established a settlement around the beginning of the 11th century, and Arab Muslim merchants and traders were settling during the 12th century.

Bantu-speaking Africans moved to Comoros from what is now southern Mozambique before the 14th century. Some African chiefs established settlements on Njazidja and Mzwani, and by the 15th century they were in contact with Arabs.

In the 15th and 16th centuries, Shirazi Arabs, who originated from the city of Shiraz in what is now Iran, arrived in the Comoros. They divided Njazidja into eleven sultanates and Nzwani into two, built mosques, and established Islam as the religion of the island. By the 16th century, the Comoros were an important trade center, exporting rice, spices, and slaves in exchange for cotton cloth and other items.

Slave trade

Competition for trade led to rivalry and warfare between the sultanates, which lasted until the French occupation in 1886. By the early 1600s, slaves were the most lucrative source of wealth. In 1785 the Sakalava of the west coast of Madagascar began slaving raids on Comoros, capturing thousands of inhabitants and taking them off in outrigger canoes to be sold in Madagascar, Mauritius, or Réunion to work on sugar plantations. Despite pleas for help to the French and other European powers, the raids continued until the Merina conquered the Sakalava kingdoms. Comoran traders then returned to trading slaves, making huge profits. A highly stratified society developed with an upper elite consisting of the sultans, a middle-class of free people, and a slave class.

Colonialism

The Portuguese were the first Europeans to arrive in the Comoros, in about 1505, and the islands first appear on a European map in 1527. The Dutch also came and their 16th-century accounts describe the Comoros trading with the African coast and Madagascar. The French arrived in the Indian Ocean in the early 17th century but it was not until 1843 that they annexed the island of Mayotte. They gained control over the other three islands in 1886 and, in 1908, the four Comoros Islands became part of France's colony of Madagascar.

Under colonial rule, slavery was brought to an end, but there were serious social and economic difficulties and wide gaps between rich and poor. The French set up crop plantations but most profits were diverted to France, or used to develop Madagascar. As a result, many Comorans emigrated to Madagascar.

Independence

In 1947 the Comoros became an overseas territory of France and, in 1960, the islands became internally self-governing. During the 1970s the French government decided that the islanders should vote to determine their status. The three western islands voted for independence; Mayotte remained under French rule.

Enslaved

This illustration is based on one made by the British explorer, David Livingstone, c.1870. It shows a mixture of male and female slaves being brutally shepherded towards the coast by their Arab captors.

Comoros: toward independence	
400s CE	Indonesian settlers arrive in the Comoros
1100s	Muslim traders from East Africa settle
1785	Sakalava from Madagascar begin slave raids
1843	France annexes the island of Mayotte
1886	France takes control of remaining three islands
1960	Comoros gain internal self-government
1974	Anjouan, Grand Comore, and Mohéli vote for independence; Mayotte votes to remain a French colony

© DIAGRAM

EUROPEAN DOMINATION

Independent Boer republics
On the Highveld Transvaal region of what is now northeastern South Africa, several republics were established by the Boers. This map shows the situation in 1894.

Gold and diamonds
From 1850–1900 minerals were discovered in the Crown Colony of Transvaal, making it one of the richest states in Southern Africa. As a result Africans were dispossessed of their lands, and forced to work as migrant laborers in the harsh environment of the mines.

During the latter half of the 19th century, stimulated by the discovery of gold and diamonds in the region, European powers, including Britain, Portugal, and Germany, intensified their influence in Southern Africa. Despite African resistance, by 1910 all of Southern Africa was under European control.

During the colonial period, white minority rule was established in South Africa, Southern Rhodesia (now Zimbabwe), and southwest Africa (now Namibia). The Portuguese took control of Mozambique, while what are now Lesotho, Botswana, and Swaziland became British protectorates, or colonies with some role in their own government.

South Africa

By the 1850s Britain, which already controlled Cape Colony, had annexed the Boer republic of Natalia and renamed it Natal. Britain had, however, recognized the Boer claims to the independent republics of Orange Free State and South African Republic (later Transvaal).

Anglo-Boer rivalry

Relations between the Boers and British were strained, and they became much worse after 1868 when diamonds and other valuable mineral resources were found in the region. In 1877, Britain annexed the South African Republic as the Crown Colony of Transvaal.

In 1880 the Boers rebelled against British control in the First Anglo-Boer War. A year later, in 1881, the British withdrew and the Boers exerted their control over the Africans living on the Highveld. The Boers finally subdued the Ndzundze Ndebele in 1883; they were dispossessed of their lands and forced to work for Afrikaner farmers. In 1898 Boer *kommandos* defeated the Venda chiefdoms, driving them north of the Limpopo River, and incorporated their lands into the Transvaal. In 1886 gold was discovered in the Transvaal; thousands of fortune seekers arrived in the region and the development of mining made the republic one of the richest states in South Africa. Increasing number of Africans were dispossessed of their lands and forced to work in the mines. Many became migrant laborers, subject to European pass laws, which restricted their dwelling and working rights. The British and Afrikaners competed for control of the mineral wealth.

The Second Boer War

In 1899 Boers of the Orange Free State and the South African Republic declared war on Britain. Some 500,000 British troops fought against 100,000 Boers and the war, which lasted until 1902, was characterized by Britain's adoption of a "scorched earth" policy in its attempt to destroy Boer resistance. In 1900 Britain annexed the Orange Free State and occupied Johannesburg, the center of the gold fields. The Boers continued to fight using guerrilla tactics in an attempt to preserve their independence, but they were ultimately defeated. The war ended in 1902 with a treaty that imposed British rule over Transvaal and the Orange Free State.

Thousands of Africans also fought in the war, some 10,000 of them with the British against the Boers. After the war Boer farmers returned to their lands, and black South Africans increasingly lost rights.

"Scorched earth"
Afrikaner women and children were forcibly moved to concentration camps, and their farms destroyed, in order to deny the Boer guerrillas access to food and supplies during the Second Boer War of 1899–1902.

Union of South Africa

In 1910 Britain merged the four territories – Cape Colony, Natal, Orange Free State, and Transvaal – to form the Union of South Africa, a self-governing country within the British Empire. The individual provinces could determine their own political rights.

Black South Africans had no political rights at all in Transvaal and Orange Free State, and only limited rights in Natal and Cape Colony. The total population in 1910 was about 5.3 million of whom four million were black, some 500,000 were Coloreds, and about 150,000 were Indian. Only 1.3 million were white, either Afrikaans- or English-speaking, but the white minority held all political power. In 1936 even the limited voting rights they had been granted were removed from black South Africans.

Ladysmith, South Africa, 1900
The British forces possessed much superior weaponry, such as the Maxim gun, than the Boers in the Second Boer War, which gave them a major advantage in the conflict.

©DIAGRAM

Southwest Africa

Colonial expansion

This map shows the situation in 1910. Major influences were the Portuguese in the late 15th century, the Dutch and English in the 17th and early 19th centuries, and the Germans and French in the late 19th century.

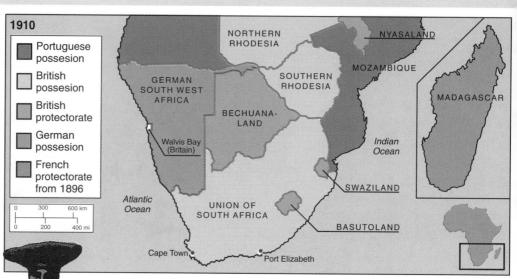

1910

- Portuguese possesion
- British possesion
- British protectorate
- German possesion
- French protectorate from 1896

0   300   600 km
0   200   400 mi

NORTHERN RHODESIA

NYASALAND

MOZAMBIQUE

GERMAN SOUTH WEST AFRICA

SOUTHERN RHODESIA

MADAGASCAR

BECHUANA-LAND

Walvis Bay (Britain)

Indian Ocean

Atlantic Ocean

SWAZILAND

UNION OF SOUTH AFRICA

BASUTOLAND

Cape Town

Port Elizabeth

The Portuguese arrived in what is now Namibia in the late 15th century. The Dutch and English explored the coast between the 17th and early 19th centuries. More European traders, explorers and missionaries entered what is now Namibia in the 19th century. They encountered the Herero, who herded long-horned cattle in the central area.

Spurred on by the race for African colonies, and in competition with colonial powers, such as Britain, Germany proclaimed the area a colony in 1884, giving it the name German Southwest Africa. Their claim included the Herero's territory. The small enclave of Walvis Bay, which the British had annexed in 1876, remained a British possession.

Herero women (above)

They adopted the distinctive clothing style of the wives of the Christian, German missionaries who came to Namibia in the 19th century. This style can still be seen today in parts of the country.

A work detail (right)

African prisoners in German Southwest Africa in the late 19th century.were chained together to prevent escape when they were marched to their place of work.

Colonial rule

German colonial rule was harsh. In the 1890s German settlers increasingly forced the Khoikhoi and Herero people out of the region, seizing Herero grazing land and confiscating their cattle when they attempted to live on the German-acquired lands. In 1904 the Herero rose up against German control, but the uprising was put down brutally with the loss of many thousands of lives. The Herero were virtually exterminated, survivors trekking into the desert regions of what is now Botswana. The area of Southwest Africa also included Ovambo territory, but this was largely ignored by the German colonizers.

South African rule

During World War I (1914–1918) South African troops occupied Southwest Africa and, in 1920, the League of Nations (the forerunner of the United Nations) gave the South African government the right to rule South West Africa, including Ovamboland. The South Africans put down Ovambo rebellions during the 1920s and 1930s. After World War II (1939–1945), the United Nations refused South Africa's request to annex the territory. Despite this, South Africa maintained its influence over Namibia and, in 1948, introduced apartheid (separatist) policies into the country. International disputes over the status of Namibia continued for many years to come.

Uprising of the Herero and Nama
Following the defeat of the Herero people of central Namibia at the hands of German troops in January 1904, the Nama herdsmen of southern Namibia rebelled in October later that year. Defeated, they too were sent to forced labor camps alongside the Herero survivors.

Collaborator
Hendrik Witbooi, a former collaborator with the Germans against the Herero people, subsequently led the Nama herdsmen against German rule. After a long, bitter struggle he was killed in battle in 1905.

©DIAGRAM

Rhodesia

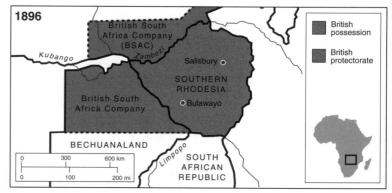

British expansion (right)
This map shows the extent of British involvement in the region surrounding what was then known as Southern Rhodesia in 1896, and is now called Zimbabwe.

"From the Cape to Cairo"
A cartoon from the early 20th century satirizes Cecil Rhodes' ambition to unify Africa using a telegraph line that would run from north to south. His main sphere of influence was Southern Africa. The Rhodesian colonies were named for him.

Shona resistance (right)
In 1890s the British South Africa Company (BSAC), headed by Cecil Rhodes, was victorious in several uprisings in southern Africa. One such rebellion was that led by the Shona people in July, 1896. The area they occupied became known as Rhodesia; the territory was further divided into Southern and Northern Rhodesia in 1897.

The area that is now Zimbabwe was colonized during the 19th century. As elsewhere, potential wealth from mineral resources was a major attraction. In 1888 the British South Africa Company (BSAC), headed by British imperialist Cecil Rhodes, obtained mineral rights from Lobengula, king of the Matabele.

The Shona resisted the British colonialists but, during the 1890s, the BSAC defeated African uprisings and seized control over an area that they named Rhodesia, for Cecil Rhodes. In 1897 the territory was divided into Southern Rhodesia (present-day Zimbabwe) and Northern Rhodesia (now Zambia).

White minority rule

White settlers were encouraged and colonized the region during the late 19th and early 20th centuries. In 1923 Southern Rhodesia became a self-governing British colony. The white minority government passed a number of laws that discriminated against the black majority. The Matabele experienced years of oppression, and white Rhodesians acquired considerable wealth at the expense of black Africans who were denied human rights and exploited for their labor. In 1953, Britain merged Southern and Northern Rhodesia and Nyasaland (now Malawi) to form the Central African Federation (CAF). In 1963 the Federation disbanded owing primarily to African resistance.

In 1964 Southern Rhodesia became known as Rhodesia, although its name was not officially changed until 1965, when a new government, led by Ian Smith, declared Rhodesia independent from Britain, in what was known as the Unilateral Declaration of Independence (UDI). Under Ian Smith, the Rhodesian government followed racist policies similar to those in South Africa.

On guard (above)
This is a sergeant from the Rhodesia Regiment standing outside the drill hall at Salisbury (now Harare) in Southern Rhodesia. The regiment was formed from members of the Southern Rhodesia Volunteers, and a number of citizens in the larger towns in the area.

Unilateral Declaration of Independence (above)
Ian Smith became prime minister of Rhodesia in 1964 and, in 1965, illegally declared independence from Britain. Civil war ensued, and Smith left office in 1979 when a non-racial government was established.

Taking up arms (below)
Female supporters of Ian Smith's white minority government in Rhodesia were prepared to take up arms to protect both themselves and his regime against opposition forces in 1965.

©DIAGRAM

High Commission Territories

David Livingstone
Both missionary and explorer, he encouraged European trade, and the spread of Christianity, in 19th-century Africa.

Gold mining
Gold was discovered in Bechuanaland (now Botswana) in the mid-19th century. Following the mining operation, the gold could be used for making currency, such as the *krugerrand*, a South African coin.

Two queens
Queen Victoria and Queen Elizabeth II are shown together on a stamp, issued in 1960, to celebrate the 75th anniversary of the Bechuanaland Protectorate.

In 1906 three colonies came under the control of the British High Commission: Bechuanaland (now Botswana), Basutoland (now Lesotho), and Swaziland.

Bechuanaland

European colonizers arrived in what is now Botswana during the 19th century. British missionaries and explorers were the first to arrive in about 1801, and encountered the Tswana. By 1817 missionaries had set up a permanent mission station at Kuruman. The Tswana's first dealings with the European explorers and missionaries were peaceful but conflict developed later in the century. In the 1830s invading Ndebele and Kololo people arrived in the region fleeing Zulu expansion, and a series of devastating civil wars occurred. In the 1860s the Tswana appealed to Britain for assistance.

During this period gold was discovered in the region and, by the late 1860s, white prospectors were flooding in. Afrikaners and the British occupied the Tswana territory and competed for control of the region. In 1885, the British divided the Tswana lands between South Africa and Britain, and, with the agreement of Khama III and other chiefs, made what is now Botswana a British colony named Bechuanaland. In 1895 Tswana chiefs ceded land to the British South Africa Company (BSAC) for railroad construction.

For many years, South Africa continued to press for Bechuanaland to be transferred to South African control but Britain refused the demands.

Basutoland

During the mid-19th century, the Basotho people, in what is now Lesotho, faced attacks from Boers seeking to take over the landlocked region. In 1868 the Basotho leader, Moshoeshoe, asked Britain for protection and the territory, known as Basutoland, became a British colony. In 1871 Basutoland was put under the administration of Cape Colony, later a province of South Africa. Following the so-called Gun War (1880–1881), Basutoland again became a British colony in 1884. Whites were forbidden to own land, and the Britain reaffirmed that the Basotho would remain independent of South African control.

In 1910 when Britain created the Union of South Africa, Basutoland was excluded from the Union and remained outside the Union, despite many attempts by South Africa to incorporate the territory. Also in 1910, Basotho chiefs and elected members set up the Basutoland Council, which remained the national law-making council until independence in 1966.

Swaziland

In the 1830s Boers and British traders reached Swaziland. Gold was discovered in the region during the late 1870s, and hundreds of prospectors arrived seeking mining concessions from the Swazi king, Mbadenzi. The Swazi kings maintained friendly relations with the Boers and granted concessions but, as a result, lost their land, resources, and ultimately their independence. In 1890, their country came under the provisional administration of the Boers. Britain and the Afrikaner Transvaal set up a provisional government, which included British, Boer, and Swazi representatives. Three years later, Britain allowed the Transvaal to administer Swaziland but not to incorporate the territory into the Transvaal. The Swazi refused to sign the agreement but, in 1895, it was allowed to rule Swaziland as a colony.

In 1902, following the Boer defeat in the Anglo-Boer War, Britain took control of Swaziland and, in 1906, it passed under the control of the British High Commission, together with the British colonies of Bechuanaland and Basutoland. Collectively, the three colonies became known as the High Commission Territories.

Paul Kruger
He was president of the Republic of Transvaal from 1883–1902. A strong and forceful champion of Afrikaner interests, he strove hard throughout his presidency to free Transvaal from British domination.

Swazi deputation to London, 1925
The king of Swaziland, Sobhuza II, and some supporters visited London to appeal to the Privy Council over a decision made about land ownership.

© DIAGRAM

79

Mozambique

Fortifications
When the Portuguese set up trading bases and settlements in Mozambique they also built many fortresses along the neighboring coastline to protect their interests.

Ngoni warriors
Adopting fighting tactics perfected by the Zulu, the Ngoni raided a number of coastal settlements controlled by the Portuguese in Southern Africa.

At the end of the 19th century, Mozambique was officially made a colony ruled from Lisbon, the Portuguese capital. Portuguese influence there had been strong for almost 400 years before, however. The Portuguese first reached the coast in the 1490s, where they subsequently attacked existing Arab trading posts and established settlements and trading bases.

In 1508 the Portuguese founded the city of Moçambique. They then established slave-trading links with the Tsonga people, who had set up kingdoms in the southeast, and began to extend their control inland along the Zambezi River. Portuguese missionaries arrived in the region during the 1680s. In the 1690s, the Changimires attacked Portuguese settlements.

Ngoni resistance

During the 19th century, the Rozvi empire collapsed and powerful Ngoni kingdoms developed in its place. The Ngoni adopted Zulu fighting tactics and raided Portuguese coastal settlements. By the 1830s, they had established a powerful military empire, Gaza, which was a major barrier to European colonial ambitions and slowed down the Portuguese takeover of the interior.

Portuguese East Africa

Initially the Portuguese developed Mozambique using a land grant system known as *prazo*, by which huge estates were granted or leased to estate holders called *prazeros*, who were virtually self-governing. They were given complete control over all the people and resources in their territory, and had their own armies to defend themselves against African chiefs. They also made use of forced labor and ignored human rights.

In 1885, European powers embroiled in the race to obtain African colonies recognized Mozambique as a Portuguese colony. Under colonial rule, the country was known as Portuguese East Africa and was ruled directly from Lisbon. In the 1890s chartered companies were set up to grow sugar and cotton for export; despite a Native Labor Code which had been introduced in 1878, the companies were even less concerned with African human rights than the *prazeros*. Thousands of Africans fled to neighboring countries.

The chartered companies were subsequently dissolved and, from the 1920s, Portugal introduced the *assimilado* system, which encouraged some Africans to gain Portuguese citizenship. Those who did not do so were severely discriminated against. In 1950 Mozambique became an overseas province of Portugal.

Forced labor
A trader leads a group of African slaves, chained together at the neck with a single beam of wood. Despite the introduction of labor codes, there was still widespread abuse of basic human rights by the colonizers.

European involvement in Southern Africa

1801–1840s	Missionaries active, Botswana
1867	Diamonds discovered near Kimberley, South Africa
1868	German missionaries and farmers settle Namibian coast
1869	Britain creates Basutoland Protectorate, Lesotho
1871	Britain annexes diamond fields, South Africa
1876	Britain annexes Walvis Bay
1877	Britain annexes Transvaal, South Africa
1878	Europeans arrive in Swaziland after gold discovered
1880–1881	Anglo-Boer War: Transvaal Boers rebel against British
1883–1884	Zulu Civil War follows British partition of Zululand
1883–1902	Paul Kruger is president of Transvaal Republic
1884	Germany colonizes South West Africa (present-day Namibia)
1885	Bechuanaland becomes a British colony
1885	Zululand divided between Britain and Transvaal
1886	Gold rush begins at Witwatersrand, South Africa
1890	British South Africa Company (BSAC) colonizes Southern Rhodesia
1891	International treaties agree borders of Mozambique
1895	Madagascar becomes a French colony
1895	Tswana chiefs cede land to BSAC for railroad construction
1897	Rhodesia divided into Northern and Southern Rhodesia
1889–1902	Anglo-Boer War: British defeat Boers
1910	Union of South Africa formed
1912	Afrikaner National Party (NP) and South African National Native Congress (SANNC) formed
1914–1918	World War I: German colonies transferred to South Africa
1920	Zululand joins South Africa
1923	SANNC becomes African National Congress (ANC); Southern Rhodesia becomes a self-governing British colony
1928	Zulu nationalist movement — Inkatha — formed
1939–1945	World War II: manufacturing boom in South Africa
1948	Apartheid policies initiated in South Africa
1953	Southern and Northern Rhodesia and Nyasaland unite to form Central African Federation (CAF)
1965	UDI: Ian Smith declares Rhodesia independent of Britain

The "Star of Africa"
A part of the world's largest uncut diamond

Orange Free State
A 1868 stamp issued during independence.

South African leaders
A stamp depicting six former prime ministers 1910–1960.

© DIAGRAM

Resistance and repression

As the Boers made inroads into Southern Africa and European powers colonized the region, they encountered resistance. At different times during the 19th and early 20th centuries, various African groups either resisted colonial expansion, or rebelled against European rule once it had been established. Either way, many of the rebellions were severely repressed, particularly the Herero rebellion in what is now Namibia.

Resistance

During the 1830s, Boers trekking into the interior met fierce resistance from various Bantu-speaking African groups, including the Xhosa, the Ndebele, and the Zulu. In 1876 the Boers assembled 5,000 troops to battle with the Pedi – the most dominant of the northern Sotho – but failed to defeat them. It was not until 1879 that a joint Swazi-British force was successful, and the once-powerful Bapedi kingdom was incorporated into the Transvaal.

Ready for battle
Many Zulu states organized their warriors into age-regiments. These provided workers and/or fighting forces, whichever were needed.

Rebellion, borders, and battles
This map of Southern Africa details the location of the various peoples, and the dates when they either resisted, or rebelled against, European expansion during the period 1650–1917. Colonial borders in 1900, and sites and dates of major battles, are also shown.

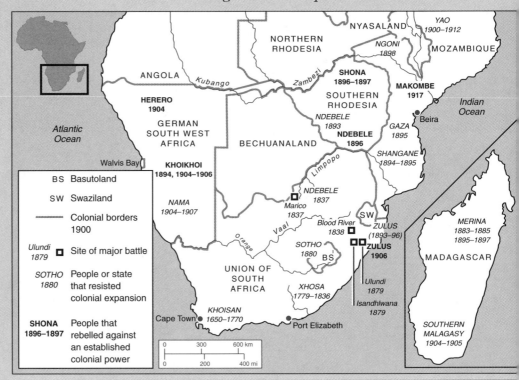

BS	Basutoland
SW	Swaziland
---	Colonial borders 1900
Ulundi 1879 ☐	Site of major battle
SOTHO 1880	People or state that resisted colonial expansion
SHONA 1896–1897	People that rebelled against an established colonial power

NYASALAND
YAO 1900–1912
NORTHERN RHODESIA
NGONI 1898
MOZAMBIQUE
ANGOLA
Kubango
Zambezi
SHONA 1896–1897
SOUTHERN RHODESIA
MAKOMBE 1917
Indian Ocean
HERERO 1904
GERMAN SOUTH WEST AFRICA
NDEBELE 1893
GAZA 1895
Beira
Atlantic Ocean
BECHUANALAND
NDEBELE 1896
Walvis Bay
KHOIKHOI 1894, 1904–1906
Limpopo
SHANGANE 1894–1895
NAMA 1904–1907
NDEBELE 1837
Marico 1837
Orange
Vaal
Blood River 1838
SW
ZULUS (1893–96)
MERINA 1883–1885 1895–1897
SOTHO 1880
BS
ZULUS 1906
MADAGASCAR
UNION OF SOUTH AFRICA
Ulundi 1879
Isandhlwana 1879
XHOSA 1779–1836
KHOISAN 1650–1770
Cape Town
Port Elizabeth
SOUTHERN MALAGASY 1904–1905

| 0 | 300 | 600 km |
| 0 | 200 | 400 mi |

In the late 19th century, the dominant people in what is now Zimbabwe were the Ndebele (Matabele). They offered fierce resistance to British colonists but, in 1893, were defeated by the British South Africa Company (BSAC) and their land, Matabeleland, became part of Southern Rhodesia. Other uprisings occurred in the same region, also in protest against the extension of European influence, including the Shona rebellion of 1896. It was put down brutally and many Shona were executed.

The Herero rebellion

One of the most bitter and savagely-repressed rebellions occurred in 1904 in German South West Africa (Namibia). German rule in South West Africa has been described as the most brutal in the whole of the continent. In 1904 the Herero people of central Namibia, led by Samuel Maherero, rose up against their German rulers. Maherero clearly stated that only German soldiers and male settlers should be attacked, and that women, missionaries, English, and Afrikaners should be left alone. A German army was sent in and the Herero warriors were no match for the superior German weapons. Maherero and his followers were forced to flee into the Kalahari Desert; those who returned were shot. The

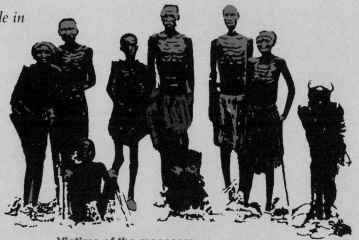

Victims of the massacre
German colonial forces massacred the Herero people following a revolt in 1904. More than three-quarters died as a result of the massacres; the remainder were either killed outright, or later died from starvation.

Germans were ordered to wipe out the Herero and, over the next six months, until the genocide ended, thousands of Herero were shot, poisoned, or died from thirst and starvation. Their population was decimated: from an estimated population of between 76,000–90,000, less than 20,000 survived.

Later, the Nama of southern Namibia also rebelled. Their rebellion, too, was brutally crushed by some 14,000 German troops. Thousands of Nama died. Those captured were sent to forced labor camps where they, in turn, died in their thousands.

Resistance to European domination

1837 Ndebele fight Boers at Marico but are defeated	**1895** Gaza resists Portuguese
1838 Battle of Blood River: British defeat Zulus	**1896** Ndebele rebel against British
1876 Pedi defeat Boers	**1896–1897** Shona rebellion against British
1879 Zulu defeat British at Isandhlwana, but are defeated by British at Ulundi	**1900–1912** Yao resist Portuguese, Mozambique
1880–1881 "Gun War:" Sotho rebellion against British defeated	**1904–1905** Herero uprising brutally suppressed
	1904–1906 Khoikhoi rebel against Germans
1893–1896 Zulus resist British	**1906** Zulus rebel against British
1893 Ndebele resist British	**1912** South African National Native Congress (SANNC) formed, it becomes African National Congress (ANC) in 1923
1894–1895 Shangane resist Portuguese	
1894 Khoikhoi rebel against Germans	**1917** Makombe revolt against Portuguese

© DIAGRAM

THE APARTHEID YEARS

"Architect of apartheid"
Dr H.F. Verwoerd was minister of "native affairs" from 1950–1958, and prime minister from 1958 until his assassination in 1966. He was responsible for developing, and ruthlessly applying, strict *apartheid* policies with the help of the then prime minister, Johannes Strijdom, whom he succeeded.

In 1948 the Afrikaner National Party won the elections in South Africa and immediately introduced apartheid (an Afrikaans word meaning "apartness"). The policy, which was based on discrimination against black South Africans, continued until 1991. It had profound effects on all aspects of life in South Africa, as well as affecting neighboring countries.

Background to apartheid

Apartheid was formally introduced in 1948, but its roots stretched back some 300 years to the arrival of Dutch settlers. From the very first, relations between the Europeans and indigenous Africans were unequal. Many of the early arrivals regarded the Africans as less than human and, as the Boers expanded their farms, they seized cattle and land from the local Khoikhoi. They also established semi-slave relationships with the local people, using them for labor and, by dispossessing them of their lands, forcing them to become dependent on the Afrikaners for their livelihood.

Afrikaner self-determination

In 1806 the British finally took Cape Colony from the Dutch and, a year later, banned the slave trade, although not slavery itself. In 1820 some 4,000 Britons settled in the Cape. Needing a labor force, the British appropriated African slaves from the Boers. In 1833 the British banned slavery throughout the British Empire.

Resentful of British control, and changes in the slave laws, the Boers began their Great Trek in 1835. They aimed to set up independent republics where they would be free of British rules. Strict Calvinists, the Boers believed they were God's chosen people and superior to the indigenous black population. Their republics had constitutions based on the right of Afrikaner self-government and their "right" to rule the "natives." Their beliefs helped to fuel extreme Afrikaner nationalism.

Union of South Africa

Following the discovery of immense gold and diamond reserves in the 1860s and 1880s, the British moved to take over the whole of South Africa. After a bitter conflict, the British defeated the Boers in the Second Anglo-Boer War (1899–1902), but British treatment of Afrikaners caused concern in Britain and there was a move towards easing the tension between them. The Afrikaner republics became self-governing colonies and, in 1910, the British and the Afrikaner colonies were merged to form the Union of South Africa. Louis Botha, an Afrikaner, was the first prime minister.

White-minority rule

Africans had fought in the Anglo-Boer War, some 10,000 of them with the British, because they believed that doing so would improve their conditions. This did not happen. Instead, Afrikaners and British were temporarily reconciled at great cost to black rights.

White minority rule was the basis of the new Union. Within the former Boer republics, blacks had no voting rights at all. Within the former British colonies, particularly Cape Colony, blacks had limited voting rights, which were subsequently removed. In practice, it meant that the white population (Afrikaans- or English-speaking) of 1.3 million had total political control over a black population of four million (1910 figures).

Despite tensions between Afrikaners and British, they combined to introduce racist policies, including the Native Lands Act of 1913, which confined blacks to "reserves" and would be the basis for later "homelands," and the 1923 Natives (Urban) Areas Act. Both created segregation that would develop further under apartheid.

Conditions for black workers deteriorated. Most were subject to pass laws, and Africans working in mines were forced to leave their lands to live in cramped, single-sex barracks.

Checking passes
Under the apartheid policy, every black person had to carry a pass with an employer's stamp if they wished to travel through a so-called "white" town.

Homelands
Displaced Africans in the Transkei and other locations were settled in areas called homelands. These were little more than camps, and were often established without even the basic amenities.

© DIAGRAM

85

Afrikaner nationalism

Dr Daniel François Malan
Prime minister from 1948–1954, he was a staunch Afrikaner nationalist and is credited with the official introduction of apartheid in South Africa. He promoted Afrikaner interests above those of any other group in the country. His cabinet, in fact, consisted only of Afrikaners, and the only language spoken at meetings was Afrikaans.

Sympathizers
A political cartoon from the 1940s points out that the National Party in South Africa publicly sympathized with Nazi Germany.

Following the creation of the Union, tensions developed once more between the Afrikaners and British, largely because of social and economic inequality. The Afrikaners were mainly farmers or members of the urban working underclass. By contrast, the British dominated the lucrative mining industry, the skilled professions, the civil service, and the military. As a result, tensions developed between the two groups and helped to encourage the rise of Afrikaner nationalism, which was increasingly directed towards the black population.

The National Party

In 1914 the National Party (NP) was formed under J.B.M. Hertzog to promote Afrikaner rights and, in 1924, it came to power. Some years later, in 1934, the NP merged with another party to form the United Party, which worked to promote the interests of both Afrikaans- and English-speaking whites. However, a more extreme National Party, with Nazi sympathies, was resurrected by the *Broederbond*, a secret and influential nationalist party under the leadership of Dr. Daniel François Malan.

The new National Party fought the 1948 election, promising to create apartheid. The South African economy had boomed during World War II, and there had been an enormous influx of black workers into the labor force. Malan immediately introduced apartheid, promising to send black Africans into reserves, and to create a white-only economy. His intentions were welcomed by many white workers, who saw the black majority as threatening their jobs, and by mine owners and white farmers, who could continue their profitable lifestyles by exploiting the cheap pool of black workers.

The realities of apartheid

To some extent, apartheid took what Nelson Mandela called the "haphazard segregation of the past three hundred years" and enshrined it in law; this is what made apartheid so different from the racial discrimination that had preceded it. Almost immediately after assuming power, Malan's National Party introduced a series of laws which, although having their origins in the past, extended and enforced segregation to a far greater extent; the ultimate aim was to create a whites-only South Africa.

The new laws, known to opponents as "unjust laws," introduced segregation into every area of life. They divided the population into four ethnic categories: whites, Africans, Coloreds, and Indians, and, in 1953, imposed a color bar in every public place to prevent whites and blacks from mixing together for any reason at all. They also prohibited mixed marriages, and sexual liaisons between the different groups.

Later, the idea of separate development was introduced, whereby black Africans were to be confined or moved to designated areas, and were to receive separate, and inferior, schooling. Laws controlled where Africans could work and live, and ruled that all Africans must carry passes with them at all times.

Voting rights

Lack of voting rights was fundamental to apartheid. By 1948, the only people with voting rights were whites, either Afrikaans-or English-speaking. Black Africans did not have the right to vote.

In 1984, the South African government introduced a tricameral Parliament, which apparently gave Indian and "Colored" voters their own Houses of Representatives. However, the white majority still maintained power, and the move was seen as an attempt to separate Indians and "Coloreds" from Africans. The measure was in fact boycotted and most people did not use their right to vote.

Relocation

Policies were also introduced to relocate blacks to designated areas. Again, these originated in earlier policies, specifically the 1913 Native Land Act. By the 1930s, the majority black population had legal rights to only 13 percent of the land.

The 1948 Group Area Act created separate residential and business areas for each "race," and people could be forcibly moved into them. In 1953, for instance, Africans were forcibly removed from the African township of Sophiatown, Johannesburg.

The Separate Amenities Act, 1953
This Act stipulated that separate facilities had to be provided for the various races of people; these facilities included public benches, beaches, and even stairways. It was also stated that the facilities did not have to be of equal standard.

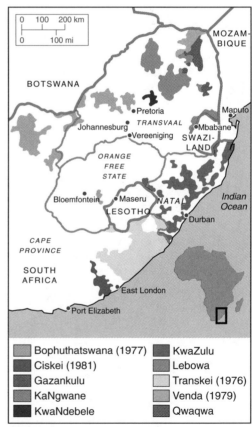

Bophuthatswana (1977)
Ciskei (1981)
Gazankulu
KaNgwane
KwaNdebele
KwaZulu
Lebowa
Transkei (1976)
Venda (1979)
Qwaqwa

Bantustans, or homelands
This map shows the location of the major homelands in Southern Africa, and the dates on which some of them were given their so-called "independence."

© DIAGRAM

Apartheid in education
Prior to the Bantu Education Act becoming law in 1953, the majority of Africans were reliant either on schools run by foreign churches, or on schools created and sponsored by missionary organizations. Either way, the children were provided a Western-style, English-language education.

Although not new, the color bar (discrimination on grounds of race) was extended under apartheid. As a result, most black South Africans were barred from skilled and professional occupations. Every South African was required to register and be classified by "race," which was then stamped on his, or her, identity pass. The pass was used to decide where they could live, who they could marry, and what job they could do.

Bantu education

Apartheid also applied to education. The 1953 Bantu Education Act denied most black students the right to a higher-standard education. Instead, they were to receive an inferior education as laid down by the Department of Native (Bantu) Affairs. Schools that refused were closed down and teachers sacked.

Resistance to *apartheid*

Early opponents of racism in South Africa included the Indian lawyer, Mohandas Karamchand Ghandi, whose non-violent tactics had a profound effect on later organizations. In 1912 a group of elite Africans formed the South African Native National Congress (SANNC), which used peaceful methods of persuasion to try and improve conditions for blacks, but without success. In 1923, it changed its name to the African National Congress (ANC).

Mass resistance emerged in the late 1940s and early 1950s, and was stimulated by the introduction of apartheid. The ANC had achieved nothing and, in 1944, Anton Lemede together with Nelson Mandela, Walter Sisulu, and Oliver Tambo formed a more radical ANC Youth League. From 1949, the ANC, under the urging of the Youth League, adopted a policy of non-violent, civil disobedience and resistance to apartheid and, for many years, spearheaded resistance. Although an all-black

TREASON TRIAL
The ACCUSED
DECEMBE 1956

Treason trial, 1956–1961
Charges against 156 people involved in the 1952 Defiance Campaign were dropped, drawing worldwide attention for the anti-apartheid campaigners.

organization, the ANC soon began to work with other organizations, both African and non-African, such as the South African Indian National Congress (SAINC), and the Communist Party of South Africa. In the end, the anti-apartheid movement included Africans, whites, Indians and "Coloreds," and support from the international community.

An early example of ANC-initiated mass mobilization was the Defiance Campaign of 1952 when trained volunteers deliberately defied apartheid laws and went to prison in their thousands. The laws were not repealed but from that point onward it was clear to the South African government that opposition existed.

Over the years, government reaction to opposition became increasingly repressive and severe. Police powers were increased, the government made use of banning, house arrest, mass imprisonment, restraining orders, surveillance, and press censorship.

Despite the increasing repression, resistance continued. The ANC, together with other organizations, maintained their commitment to non-violence. However, in 1961 Nelson Mandela and others formed *Umkhonto we Sizwe* (Spear of the Nation), which carried out sabotage acts on communication centers and other strategic targets.

By the early 1960s, the ANC had been banned and many leaders, including Nelson Mandela and Walter Sisulu, had been imprisoned for life. Oliver Tambo went into exile setting up ANC offices in Lusaka and elsewhere, and drumming up international support.

During the 1970s, a second-wave of resistance occurred when the Black Consciousness movement emerged, led by Steve Biko and others. Many were young students, who had grown up under apartheid. Huge uprisings took place in Soweto in 1976, when the government announced that Afrikaans would be used for education. Protests escalated and many hundreds were killed.

Sharpeville massacre, 1960
Sixty-nine demonstrators were killed, and over 100 injured, when the police opened fire on the crowd outside a police station in Sharpeville. Most were shot in the back.

Soweto uprisings, 1976
The distraught members of Hector Pieterson's family carry his injured body away from the carnage after policemen opened fire on a group of schoolchildren in the township of Soweto.

© DIAGRAM

The end of apartheid

On patrol
Armed police made regular patrols in the South African townships, helping to create the atmosphere of a war zone rather than a peaceful place in which people could live.

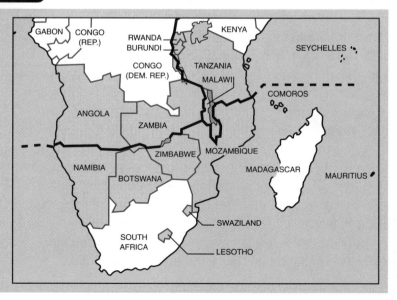

Free at last
Nelson Mandela and his then wife, Winnie, celebrate release from prison, Cape Town, February 11, 1990.

From the late 1970s, particularly after the Soweto uprisings, the South African government came under increasing pressure to end apartheid. The United Nations, the US Congress, and other members of the international community urged restraint and an end to apartheid.

In the mid-1980s, economic and other sanctions were imposed, which left South Africa largely isolated in the world. Within South Africa as well, white businesses and employers – both English and Afrikaner – were beginning to demand an end to repressive labor laws, which made skilled labor scarce. Foreign investors were pulling out, and the country was experiencing an economic slump. Violence within the townships was also escalating.

By the late 1980s, apartheid was ceasing to be workable and the South African government entered into discussions with Nelson Mandela, who was still in prison.

In 1990, the then prime minister, F.W. de Klerk, released Mandela, lifted restrictions on political organizations. By 1991, apartheid had been dismantled.

In 1994, the country's first multiracial elections were held, and Nelson Mandela became president.

Neighboring states
With its wealth and military strength, South Africa was able to dominate neighboring states. Some, known as the front-line states, opposed apartheid and South Africa used intimidation, sabotage, subversion, and military force against such countries as Angola and Mozambique to destabilize them and protect its policies. To justify invasions, South Africa used the excuse of eliminating anti-apartheid guerrilla bases. Angola was subjected to a long civil war. South Africa illegally occupied Namibia until 1990, where it introduced a form of apartheid, as well as pressurizing Lesotho and Swaziland into supporting them. The illegal white minority regime in Rhodesia (now Zimbabwe) was also propped up by South Africa.

GABON | CONGO (REP.) | RWANDA | BURUNDI | KENYA | SEYCHELLES | CONGO (DEM. REP.) | TANZANIA | MALAWI | COMOROS | ANGOLA | ZAMBIA | MOZAMBIQUE | MADAGASCAR | ZIMBABWE | NAMIBIA | BOTSWANA | MAURITIUS | SWAZILAND | SOUTH AFRICA | LESOTHO

A chronology of apartheid in Southern Africa

1652 Dutch establish first settlement in Southern Africa, Cape Colony
1785 British occupy Cape Colony
1809 First "pass law" introduced
1820 First British settlers arrive at Cape Colony
1833 Britain abolishes slavery in the Empire
1836 Boers begin Great Trek
1910 Union of South Africa created
1910 Ministry of Native Affairs set up
1912 South African Native National Congress (SANNC) formed
1913 Native Land Act restricts black South Africans to "native reserves"
1914 Pro-Afrikaner National Party (NP) formed
1914–1918 World War I. Economy booms, black South African labor force expands
1920 More than 70,000 black African miners strike for better conditions
1921 South African Communist Party formed
1923 Native (Urban Areas) Act restricts numbers of black South Africans in towns and cities
1923 SANNC becomes African National Congress (ANC)
1933 National Party (NP) merges with South African Party to form United Party
1934 Extreme Afrikaner nationalists form new National Party under D. F. Malan
1939–1945 World War II: South Africa joins war on British side; economy booms.
1944 ANC Youth League is formed
1948 Malan's National Party wins election: introduction of apartheid
1949–1953 National Party introduces series of repressive laws
1949 ANC adopts non-violent civil disobedience to oppose apartheid
1952 ANC launches Defiance Campaign
1953 Bantu Education sets up inferior schooling for blacks
1953 National Party begins program of forcible removal of black South Africans from Sophiatown, Johannesburg
1955 Congress of the People issues Freedom Charter
1956–1961 Treason Trial: 156 activists, including Mandela, acquitted
1958 Hendrik Verwoerd becomes Prime Minister, expands apartheid
1959 Promotion of Bantu Self-Government Act creates black "homelands" (Bantustans)
1959 Pan African Congress (PAC) formed
1960 Sharpeville Massacre. ANC and PAC banned
1961 *Umkhonto we Sizwe* (Spear of the Nation) begins armed struggle
1961 South Africa becomes republic
1962–1963 Government introduces anti-sabotage, 90-day detention and other repressive measures
1963 Rivonia Trial: Mandela and other anti-apartheid leaders imprisoned for life
1976 Soweto uprising: police kill schoolchildren
1977 Gleneagles Agreement, advocating international sports ban on South Africa
1980 Free Mandela Campaign begins
1981 South Africa launches military force against ANC offices, Mozambique
1983 Tricameral Parliament set up
1983 United Democratic Front (UDF) formed
1986 South African government attacks ANC bases in Botswana, Zambia, and Zimbabwe. State of Emergency introduced. Economic sanctions imposed.
1987 Talks begin between government and Mandela
1990 ANC, PAC and other organizations unbanned; Mandela released
1990–1991 Government repeals apartheid laws
1994 First multiracial elections held in South Africa

© DIAGRAM

LIBERATION MOVEMENTS

Toivo Herman Ja Toivo
A colleague of Sam Nujoma's, he helped to found the South West African People's Organization (SWAPO) in Cape Town in 1959. The movement initially grew out of the disaffection of migrant workers, and later became the chief nationalist group.

Following the imposition of white minority rule in what are now Namibia, South Africa, Zimbabwe, and Mozambique, liberation movements sprang up to fight for change. The liberation struggles lasted for many years and often involved bitter and brutal guerrilla warfare.

Namibia

In 1915 German South West Africa together with Ovamboland came under South African administration. The Ovambo rebelled in the 1920s and 1930s but were defeated and, in 1948, South Africa introduced its apartheid policies into the country, effectively making Namibia South Africa's fifth province in 1949. Despite protests by the Ovambo and the international community, it was made an "independent" homeland. The Ovambo were only allowed to leave with a pass, and also without members of their family.

Sam Nujoma
A cofounder of SWAPO in 1959, from 1966 he led a guerrilla war against the occupation of Namibia by South Africa. He became president in 1990, and was reelected in 1994 and 1999.

In 1958 the Ovambo formed the Ovamboland People's Party to resist South African rule. In 1960 it became the South West Africa People's Organization (SWAPO), led by Sam Nujoma. Launched by Ovambo contract workers, and influenced by South African liberation organizations, SWAPO ultimately represented most southwest Africans in their opposition to apartheid and subordination to South Africa. Initially SWAPO attempted to negotiate with South Africa for independence but without success, and in 1966 SWAPO launched a guerrilla war against South Africa that continued well into the 1980s.

Liberation organizations

ANC African National Congress. Organization that spearheaded resistance to apartheid in South Africa
FRELIMO Front for the Liberation of Mozambique. Guerrilla movement that fought Mozambique's white government
PAC Pan-African Congress. African nationalist liberation group in South Africa
SAIC South African Indian Congress, also known as Indian Congress. Formed by Indians to fight for rights in South Africa
SWAPO South West Africa People's Organization. Led resistance against South Africa's occupation of Namibia
UDF United Democratic Front. Umbrella group consisting of more than 300 anti-apartheid organizations in South Africa
ZAPU Zimbabwe African People's Union. Nationalist movement led by Joshua Nkomo
ZANU Zimbabwe African Union. Nationalist movement led by Robert Mugabe from 1976

The ANC
The flag of the African National Congress.

SWAPO's struggle was backed by the international community. In 1966, the United Nations (UN) voted to end South African rule, and two years later, following a request from SWAPO, renamed the country Namibia. In 1971, the International Court of Justice declared that South Africa's occupation of Namibia was illegal.

Despite this, South African occupation continued. In 1974 SWAPO set up guerrilla bases in newly-independent Angola. South Africa proposed an independence plan for Namibia but, in 1978, SWAPO organized a boycott of the elections. SWAPO guerrillas continued to wage war against South Africa from their Angolan bases, and in 1989 South Africa was finally forced into a ceasefire. Free elections were held in 1990 and won by SWAPO.

Mozambique

Some of the most ferocious wars against colonialism in Africa occurred in the Portuguese colonies. Mozambique became a Portuguese overseas province in 1950. In 1960 the Mozambique Liberation Front (FRELIMO) was launched, headed by Eduardo Mondlane, a Mozambican intellectual living in Dar es Salaam. From that point FRELIMO led the struggle against white colonial rule. In 1964 FRELIMO launched a guerrilla war against military targets in northern Mozambique, and soon claimed to have established control in the northern districts. Portuguese troops, aided by the state security police (PIDE) fought with FRELIMO members, and villagers supporting the nationalists were subject to savage reprisals.

In 1969 Mondlane was assassinated and Marxist Samora Machel became FRELIMO president. The Portuguese attempted to contain the liberation movement in the north, and to make use of ethnic rivalries, but FRELIMO gained support and, in 1974, their struggle was aided by a military coup in Portugal which ousted the authoritarian government of Marcello Caetano. The new military regime of Portugal negotiated Mozambique's independence with FRELIMO, which was achieved in 1975.

Freedom fighter (left)
This woman is typical of those who fought in the war for liberation from Portuguese colonial rule in Mozambique. FRELIMO, the Liberation Front, was formed in 1960 in Dar es Salaam by Mozambican Eduardo Mondlane.

Victory march (below)
Based on a mural which is housed in the Maputo Museum in Mozambique, this illustration vividly captures the revolutionary zeal of the FRELIMO freedom fighters, and the support they enjoyed.

© DIAGRAM

93

The struggle in South Africa and Zimbabwe

An act of defiance
Members of the Pan African Congress (PAC), formed in 1959, burn pass books (restricting their freedom of movement) in an act of non-violent civil disobedience against white rule in South Africa.

Opposition to white rule in South Africa began as early as 1912 with the formation of the South African Native National Congress (SANNC), renamed the African National Congress (ANC) in 1923. Resistance grew after 1948 when the National Party (NP) was elected to power with a white-only electorate, and introduced apartheid. The ANC, which included leaders such as Nelson Mandela, Oliver Tambo, and Walter Sisulu, led black opposition to apartheid policies, particularly during the 1950s, but worked in alliance with many other organizations, including the South African Indian Congress (SAIC), the South African Colored People's Organization (SACPO), the Congress of Democrats (COD), and the Communist Party of South Africa. In 1955 this Congress Alliance drew up the Freedom Charter, a program of nonracial social democracy and a blueprint for a multiracial South Africa. Other African nationalists formed the Pan-African Congress (PAC) in 1959.

Initial tactics in the struggle were based on nonviolent civil disobedience, and continued to be a feature of the liberation movement throughout its history. However, from 1960, various individuals and organizations, notably *Umkhonto we Sizwe* (Spear of the Nation), adopted sabotage and armed struggle.

By 1963, most leaders of the liberation struggle within South Africa had either been imprisoned, or driven into exile. The ANC and other opposition groups had also been declared illegal. The ANC, under Oliver Tambo, set up headquarters and bases outside the country, notably in Angola and Mozambique which offered support. During the 1970s a second-wave liberation struggle emerged in South Africa with the rise of Black Consciousness, a black nationalist movement, which included such leaders as Steve Biko, who was killed in police custody in 1977.

Silkscreen poster, 1986 Between 1948–1991 much South African art highlighted both the injustices and the inequalities of the apartheid system.

HOW LONG MUST WE KEEP ON DYING IN THIS WAY?

Ultimately, the anti-apartheid movement included peoples and groups from all ethnic groups – black, Colored, Asian, and liberal whites – all of which strongly opposed the discriminatory policies of South Africa.

The more repressive the measures the South African government used to shore up their policies, the greater the support for the liberation movement from the international community. While resistance continued in South Africa, international organizations such as the Commonwealth, the European Union (EU), and the United Nations added pressure in the form of sanctions.

Ultimately, the South African government had to talk with the ANC and apartheid came to an end in 1991; the first free and multiracial elections were held in 1994.

Zimbabwe

The liberation movement in what is now Zimbabwe was closely linked to liberation struggles in Mozambique. In 1965 the Rhodesian Front (RF) party under Ian Smith unilaterally declared Rhodesia (now Zimbabwe) independent. Less than one percent of black Rhodesians were allowed to vote. Successive nationalist organizations were banned, and their leaders detained or exiled.

However, by 1966 two major nationalists groups emerged: the Zimbabwe African People's Union (ZAPU) under Joshua Nkomo, and the Zimbabwe African National Union (ZANU), led from 1976 by Robert Mugabe. They entered into guerrilla war against government troops and, following FRELIMO's success in northern Mozambique in 1970–1971, began to make a significant amount of headway.

War continued throughout the 1970s. By 1978 it was obvious that the Rhodesian government would not win the war and Smith, under pressure from the international community, agreed to multi-racial elections in 1979. However, ZAPU and ZANU were excluded, and guerrilla warfare continued. In 1979 negotiations led to a peace settlement and, in 1980, Mugabe and ZANU won an electoral victory.

Steve Biko
A leader of the Black Consciousness Movement that emerged in the 1970s in South Africa, Biko was arrested in 1977 and later died in police custody. He believed that oppression had convinced many blacks that they were inferior to whites, and sought to restore pride in being black.

A history of resistence movements

1928	Zulu nationalist movement, Inkatha, formed
1944	ANC Youth League formed
1952	ANC initiates Defiance Campaign, South Africa
1958	Ovamboland People's Organization formed, Namibia
1960	SWAPO founded, Namibia
1960	National Democratic Party (NDP) formed, Rhodesia
1961	FRELIMO formed, Mozambique
1961	*Umkhonto we Sizwe* formed, South Africa
1963	NDP splits into Zimbabwe African Peoples' Union (ZAPU) and Zimbabwe African National Union (ZANU)
1964	FRELIMO gains control of northern Mozambique
1966	SWAPO rebels confront South African forces
1967–1975	Guerrillas fight against white Rhodesians, Zimbabwe
1970s	Black Consciousness movement active, South Africa
1973	UN recognizes SWAPO as representative of Namibia
1976	ZAPU and ZANU join to form Patriotic Front (PF), Zimbabwe
1983	United Democratic Front (UDF) formed in South Africa

© DIAGRAM

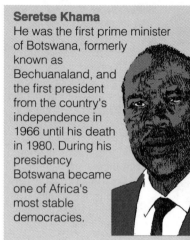

Seretse Khama
He was the first prime minister of Botswana, formerly known as Bechuanaland, and the first president from the country's independence in 1966 until his death in 1980. During his presidency Botswana became one of Africa's most stable democracies.

Between 1960 and the early 1990s all the countries of Southern Africa achieved independence from colonial or white-minority rule. Since then their fortunes have varied. South Africa has remained the most powerful and economically developed country in the region. Following the end of apartheid, and the adoption of a multi-racial democracy in the early 1990s, the country worked to achieve reconciliation internally, and began to mediate in disputes outside its borders. Botswana experienced political stability and has one of the fastest-growing economies in the region. By contrast, Zimbabwe's long struggle to achieve black majority rule had, by 2000, led to violence and bloodshed. Madagascar and Mozambique remained the poorest countries in the region. By 2002 the world's greatest explosion of HIV infection was affecting the whole region, while Lesotho, Mozambique, Swaziland, and Zimbabwe were facing famine and grave food shortages caused by drought and ravaged crops.

Botswana

Known then as Bechuanaland, Botswana remained a British protectorate until the 1960s. In 1961 executive and legislative councils were set up and, in 1965, a constitution was introduced which allowed for internal self-government. In 1966 the first general election took place. The Bechuanaland Democratic Party (BDP), led by Seretse Khama, a former Tswana chief, won 28 out of 31 seats in the Legislative Assembly. Botswana became an independent republic in September 1966. Khama was the first president and the Legislative Assembly became the National Council.

Despite pressure from South Africa and what was then Rhodesia (Zimbabwe), Botswana achieved a stable multi-party democracy. Khama died in 1980 and was succeeded as president by Dr Ketumile Masire, head of the BDP. He retired in 1998 and was succeeded by Festus Mogae. A year later the BDP again formed the government, winning the majority of the vote.

In 1966 Botswana was one of the poorest countries in Africa, reliant on meat and live animal exports to earn

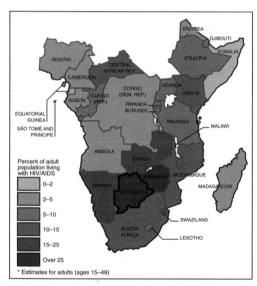

Percent of adult population living with HIV/AIDS
- 0–2
- 2–5
- 5–10
- 10–15
- 15–25
- Over 25

* Estimates for adults (ages 15–49)

The AIDS crisis in Botswana
Estimates suggest that over a quarter of the adult population of Botswana may be infected with AIDS. This is reflected in a rapidly-declining average life expectancy. Children born this century now have an average life expectancy of 40 years, rather than the 70 years predicted for those in normal health.

income for the nation. Since then mineral production, particularly of diamonds, has transformed the economy, giving it one of the highest gross national products in Africa. These developments in turn created a healthy economy that enabled Botswana to set up game reserves and national parks, which stimulated tourism.

Despite its economic growth, many people in Botswana remained poor, and by 2000 there were serious problems: high unemployment, overgrazing, and the spread of HIV/AIDS.

Comoros

In 1975 the three western Comoros Islands became independent from France. Mayotte voted to remain under French rule. Since then Comoros has experienced political and social instability, largely due to ethnic differences and political rivalries.

The first president was Abderrahman Ahmed Abdallah who, only a month after independence, was overthrown in a coup by Ali Soilih, backed by French mercenaries. Unsuccessful coups followed until 1978 when Soilih himself was overthrown and Abdallah, with French support, became president again. He set up an Islamic republic. More coups followed and, in 1989, Abdallah was assassinated. In 1990 Comoros returned to democracy; in 1996 Mohammed Taki Abdoulkarim was elected president of the island.

In 1997 Anjouan and Mohéli announced their intention to secede from the Comoros. Troops from Grande Comore attempted unsuccessfully to conquer Anjouan and, in 1998, it declared independence. The Organization of African Unity (OAU), the French government, and the Comorian government tried to restore unity. Following Taki's death in 1998, an agreement was drawn up proposing greater autonomy for the two islands. Political disruption continued into the early 21st century.

Under arrest
The mercenary leader Bob Denard was arrested in 1995 after a failed attempt to overthrow the government. This was not the first time Denard had staged a coup in Comoros: he had also led mercenary forces in 1978 who toppled Soilih and restored Abdallah to power and, in 1989, he commanded the presidential guard who assassinated Abdallah.

A wave of support
Residents of Anjouan were split in their allegiances in 1998: some supported independence from France, while others preferred to remain under its control.

© DIAGRAM

Lesotho, Madagascar and Mauritius

Letsie III
He was made king of Lesotho by the military government which ruled the country in 1990. He abdicated in 1995 to allow his father to return as king, but assumed the title again upon his father's death.

In 1960 Basutoland adopted its first constitution and, in 1964, became a constitutional monarchy. A year later the Basutoland National Party (BNP) won a narrow majority in the National Assembly. Chief Lebua Jonathan became prime minister and chief Motlotlehi Moshoeshoe II became king. In 1966 Lesotho became independent.

Since independence, Lesotho has experienced political instability. King Moshoeshoe II demanded extra powers and was placed under house arrest until he accepted a ceremonial role only. In 1970 Jonathan suspended the constitution and Moshoeshoe II left the country.

During the 1980s tensions developed between Lesotho and South Africa, when Jonathan criticized South Africa's apartheid policies and refused to hand over ANC activists resident in Lesotho. South Africa then imposed economic sanctions on Lesotho. In 1986 a military coup overthrew Jonathan. Justin Lekhanya installed Moshoeshoe's son, Letsie III, on the throne but, in 1991, was forced out of office. Ntsu Mokhehle was elected prime minister and Moshoeshoe restored to the throne in 1996. A year later he died and Letsie III again became monarch. Mokhehle formed a new party, but there was an army mutiny. South African and Botswanan troops entered the country to restore order. They withdrew in 1999. At elections in May 2002, Bethuel Mosisili's Lesotho Congress for Democracy party won 77 of 78 constituency seats and Letsie III remained head of state.

Wildcat
This is an election poster for the *Parti Social Démocrate* of Madagascar, led by Philibert Tsiranana. The first president of the newly-independent Malagasy Republic, he resigned in 1972 amid charges of electoral fraud.

Madagascar

In 1960 Madagascar became independent as the Malagasy Republic. Its first president was Philibert Tsiranana, leader of the Social Democratic Party. In 1972, charges of electoral fraud led to his resignation. A military group, led by Major General Ramanantsoa, took control and, during the mid-1970s, set about removing French military personnel and civil servants. Ramanantsoa also established contact with the Communist bloc. Didier Ratsiraka became president and head of the Revolutionary Council in 1975. In 1977 the country became a one-party state, ruled by Ratsiraka's National

Gabriel Ramanantsoa
He became president of Madagascar in 1972 following the resignation of Philibert Tsiranana. A popular leader at first, he later handed power over to the military authorities after an attempted coup.

Front for the Defense of the Revolution.

During the 1980s, economic problems led to a liberalizing of economic policies with greater emphasis on private enterprise. In 1992 a multiparty system was restored. In 1993 Albert Zafy defeated Ratsiraka to become president, but resigned in 1996 and Ratsiraka returned to office. In 2002 Ratsiraka refused to accept defeat in elections. But he finally left the country, relinquishing control to Marc Ravalomanana.

Mauritius

In 1968 Mauritius became independent as a constitutional monarchy. Between 1968–1982 the country was ruled by the Mauritius Labor Party, with Sir Seewoosagur Ramgoolam as prime minister. Although he worked to reconcile tensions and problems between different ethnic groups, he was forced to declare a state of emergency during a Muslim/Creole conflict.

Between 1969 and the early 1970s, islanders from Diego Garcia, which Britain had leased to the United States despite Mauritian authority over the island, were resettled on Mauritius. From 1982 Mauritius laid claim to the Chagos Archipelago (of which Diego Garcia is a part) and, in 2002, the British High Court ruled that Britain had acted illegally in expelling the islanders.

Following economic difficulties, Ramgoolam's government lost popularity. In 1982 the left-wing Mauritian Militant Movement (MMM) was elected to government, with Aneerood Jugnauth as prime minister. In 1983 he left the MMM and formed the Militant Socialist Movement (MSM), which in coalition with other parties, won further elections. In 1992 Jugnauth made Mauritius a republic, with Sir Cassam Uteem as president. Political power swung between the MMM and MLP until 2000 when the MMM in alliance with the MSM won the election, with Jugnauth as prime minister.

Mauritius experienced economic success throughout the 1990s but ethnic tensions continued.

Sir Seewoosagur Ramgoolam
He was the leader of the Mauritius Labor Party, and prime minister of the country from 1968–1982. Although he was generally pro-western in his political views, he opposed Britain's transfer of Diego Garcia from Mauritian authority in 1965.

The exile boat
MV Nordvaer, a small passenger and cargo vessel from Norway, was used for the deportation of the indigenous population (some 300–400 people) of Diego Garcia to Mauritius in 1972–1973.

© DIAGRAM

Frelimo poster, 1976
Led by the Front for the Liberation of Mozambique (FRELIMO), Mozambique became a one-party, Marxist state.

Following a long struggle, Mozambique achieved independence in 1975, with FRELIMO leader Samora Machel as president. Under FRELIMO, Mozambique was a one-party Marxist state. The government had problems with South Africa and what was then Rhodesia. Mozambique provided bases for Zimbabwean guerrillas fighting white minority rule in Rhodesia, which led to attacks on the country by Rhodesian and South African forces. Mozambique also provided shelter for ANC activists. As a result, South Africa backed the National Resistance Movement (RENAMO), a guerrilla force who opposed the FRELIMO government. Civil war broke out between government forces and the guerrillas, which shattered the economy and lasted until 1992 when FRELIMO and RENAMO signed a peace agreement.

In 1986 Machel died in a plane crash and Joaquim Chissano became president. During the 1980s Marxist policies were liberalized and officially ended in 1989. The first multiparty elections took place in 1994 and were won by FRELIMO, who again won a majority in the 1999 elections. During the 1990s, advised by the International Monetary Fund (IMF), Mozambique rebuilt its economy, which by 1999 was rated as the fastest growing in the world. Devastating floods in March 2000 set back the economy considerably, however.

Namibia

In 1989 South Africa agreed a ceasefire with the South West Africa People's Organization (SWAPO), which had fought a guerrilla war against South Africa for nearly 30 years. Elections held in 1989 were won by SWAPO, who gained a 41-seat majority in Namibia's National Assembly. The next year, Namibia achieved independence with Sam Nujoma as president. Nujoma and SWAPO were re-elected in 1994 and 1999, despite criticism of Nujoma's action in sending troops to support the government of Democratic Republic of Congo. In 1999 Namibian troops put down a rebellion by Lozi people, living in the Caprivi Strip, which links Namibia to northern Angola, Zambia, and Zimbabwe.

A celebration of freedom
Namibia achieved independence in 1990 as a result of a guerrilla war, lasting over 30 years, waged by the South West African People's Organization (SWAPO) against South African occupation of the country.

South Africa

Technically South Africa achieved independence in 1961 when the white minority government announced a republic and left the British Commonwealth. However, the black majority was still subject to South Africa's apartheid laws. In 1989 F.W. de Klerk became president and began talks with the African National Congress (ANC), which led to the movement being legalized, the release of Nelson Mandela, and the ending of apartheid.

The country's first multiracial elections were held in 1994. They were won by the ANC, and Nelson Mandela became president. Under Mandela, the government pursued a policy of reconciliation, and included people of different ethnic and political groups, including F.W. de Klerk. Mandela retired in 1999. The ANC again won the 1999 elections and Thabo Mbeki succeeded Mandela as president. Mbeki faced many problems. In 2000 a UN report estimated that 10 percent of South Africans were infected with HIV. Mbeki faced criticism for his failure to deal with the AIDS crisis and, in 2002, the High Court ordered the government to give antiviral agents to HIV-positive pregnant women in state hospitals.

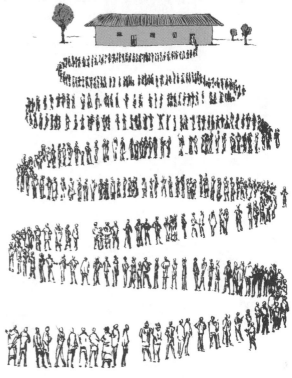

Going to the polls
Democracy and justice were finally upheld in South Africa during the first multiracial elections which were held in 1994. Long lines of patient Southern African people queued in the countryside and the cities to cast their first votes in over half a century of white-dominated rule.

Swaziland

In 1968 Swaziland achieved independence as a constitutional monarchy, with Sobhuza II as king. However, he and other Swazi leaders opposed the constitution, and since then Swaziland has been ruled as an absolute monarchy. In 1973 Sobhuza suspended the constitution, banned political parties and ruled the country directly. Following his death in 1982, one of his sons, Makhosetive, succeeded him, and was crowned as Mswati III. Mswati suspended his father's council, dismissed the prime minister and in 1992 began to rule by decree. By the mid-1990s, prodemocracy protest had emerged. Mswati set up a commission to review the constitution but it was unfairly filled with members of the royal family. Elections took place in 1998 but turnout was low. In 2002 Mswati continued to rule by decree. Swaziland was also experiencing a serious AIDS crisis.

Sobhuza II
He was made king of Swaziland in 1922 and, almost half a century later, head of state in 1968 when the country achieved independence from British control.

©DIAGRAM

101

Zimbabwe

Zimbabwe: the moves toward independence

1963 Central African Federation is dissolved
1964 Black nationalist organizations Zimbabwe African People's Union (ZAPU) and Zimbabwe African National Union (ZANU) are formed
1964 Ian Smith becomes leader of the Rhodesian Front (RF)
1965 Ian Smith issues unilateral declaration of independence (UDI)
1966 Guerrilla war begins
1976 Patriotic Front formed between Joshua Nkomo and Robert Mugabe
1980 ZANU win election. Mugabe becomes prime minister
1980 Rhodesia becomes independent as republic of Zimbabwe
1987 Mugabe becomes president
1988 Zimbabwe becomes one-party state
1991 Opposition parties legalized under restricted conditions
1992 Land Acquistion Act introduced
2000 Electors reject proposals to extend president's powers
2001 Armed squatters invade white farms
2002 Mugabe wins election despite accusations of electoral fraud

Reverend Canaan Banana (left)
A former activist in the protracted struggle for independence, he became the first president of Zimbabwe when the country achieved majority rule in November 1980.

Intimidation (below)
Robert Mugabe used military force to shore up his campaign for reelection as leader of Zimbabwe in 2001–2002.

In 1965 Ian Smith, head of the white-minority government of what was then Southern Rhodesia (now Zimbabwe), made a unilateral declaration of independence (UDI) from Britain and named the country Rhodesia. Despite his action being declared illegal, Smith's government continued to rule the country until 1980. Strongly influenced by South Africa, the Rhodesian government introduced apartheid-like policies into Rhodesia that discriminated against the black majority.

Independence

By the mid-1970s international pressure and 10 years of bitter guerrilla warfare, which caused thousands of deaths and 1 million refugees, forced the white minority government into plans to include moderate blacks in the government. Abel Muzorewa, a Methodist bishop, was elected prime minister. This did not stop the guerrilla war and, in 1980, elections were held. ZANU-PF, or the Patriotic Front, won the elections with Robert Mugabe as prime minister and head of the government. Rhodesia became independent as the Republic of Zimbabwe.

Power struggles

The early years of independence saw a political power struggle between Joshua Nkomo, who had led the former nationalist Zimbabwe African People's Union (ZAPU), and drew support from the Matabele people, and Robert Mugabe, who had led the Zimbabwe African National Union (ZANU).

In the 1980 elections Mugabe's ZANU defeated Nkomo's ZAPU. Nkomo was given a cabinet

A force for change? (below)
Morgan Tsvangirai was the leader of the opposition Movement for Democratic Change during the recent election in Zimbabwe.

Stand-off (above)
A white woman, together with infant children, is confronted by angry invaders intent on repossessing a farm.

position but was dismissed in 1982 following conflicts between the two groups. Further tensions developed when Matabeleland sheltered dissidents from Mugabe's rule. In 1985 ZANU again won the election. The office of prime minister was abolished and replaced by that of executive president. Parliament elected Mugabe to the office. In 1988 the two groups merged, making Zimbabwe effectively a one-party state. Nkomo served as a vice president until his death in 1999.

Land reform

During the colonial period white settlers had taken Zimbabwe's best farmland from the black population. A 1931 Act of Parliament had ruled that only the 48,000 white Rhodesians could own 48 million acres. By contrast, 1 million Africans were left with only 29 million acres, most of it poor land, riddled with tsetse-fly.

Following independence, land reform was a major issue and white farmers soon faced problems. In 1992 Mugabe's government passed the Land Apportionment Act and began to buy back European-owned land for redistribution to landless Africans. In 2000, however, Mugabe's government began to take over European-owned farms without paying compensation, a policy that led to violence and the murder of some farmers. The actions were widely criticized but land takeovers continued. Mugabe's government began to lose popularity, and intimidation was used to silence critics. In 2002 Mugabe was reelected president, despite allegations of vote rigging. Repossession of farms continued.

© DIAGRAM

Coups d'État in Southern Africa

Independence from colonial rule by various European powers proved difficult to achieve for many African nations. Yet, once independence had been acheived, different problems beset the new states.

As the maps (right) show, some nations were subject to political instability and military *coups d'état* after independence.

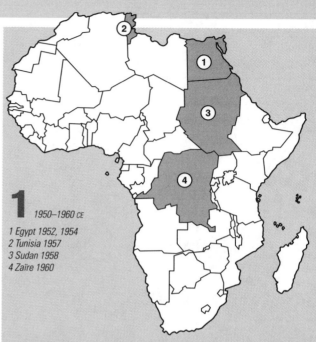

1 1950–1960 CE

1 Egypt 1952, 1954
2 Tunisia 1957
3 Sudan 1958
4 Zaïre 1960

Canaan Banana
He became the first president of Zimbabwe when the country achieved majority rule in 1980.

Steve Biko
He was the leader of the South African Black Consciousness Movement which emerged in 1970.

Seretse Khama
He served as the first president of an independent Botswana from1966 until his death in 1980.

Nelson Mandela
He was elected president of South Africa in the first non-racial elections which were held in 1994.

Sam Nujoma
He was a cofounder of SWAPO in 1959, and led a guerrilla war against South Africa's occupation of Namibia.

Sobhuza II
He was made king of Swaziland in 1922, and head of state in 1968 when it became independent of British colonial rule.

Coups d'état in Southern Africa
Successful *coup d'états* placed these leaders in power.

Ahmed Abdallah
He became president of the Comoros following a *coup d'état* in 1978 in which Ali Soilih was overthrown. Abdallah later died in another *coup* in 1989.

King Letsie III
He was made king of Lesotho in 1991 by a military government under the control of General Justin Lekhanya. He abdicated in 1995, but returned again as king in 1996.

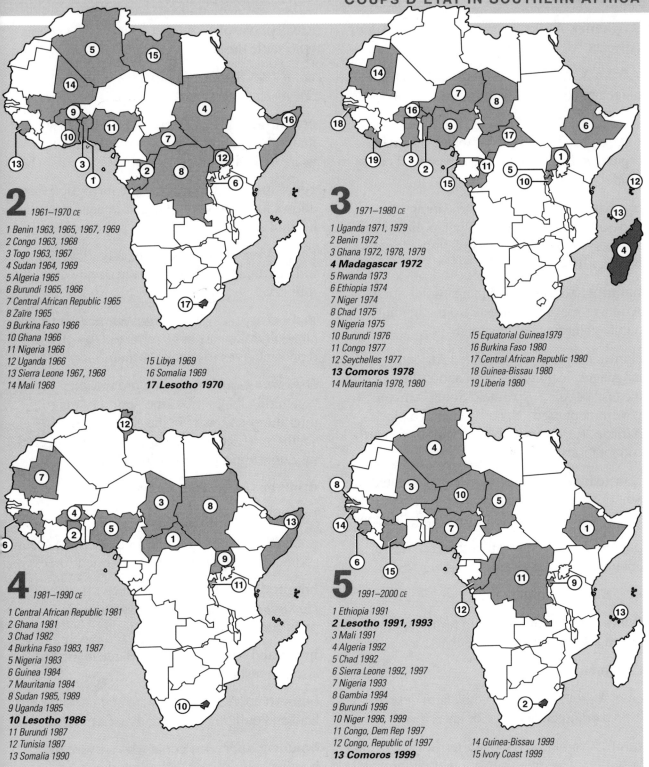

2 1961–1970 CE

1 Benin 1963, 1965, 1967, 1969
2 Congo 1963, 1968
3 Togo 1963, 1967
4 Sudan 1964, 1969
5 Algeria 1965
6 Burundi 1965, 1966
7 Central African Republic 1965
8 Zaïre 1965
9 Burkina Faso 1966
10 Ghana 1966
11 Nigeria 1966
12 Uganda 1966
13 Sierra Leone 1967, 1968
14 Mali 1968
15 Libya 1969
16 Somalia 1969
17 Lesotho 1970

3 1971–1980 CE

1 Uganda 1971, 1979
2 Benin 1972
3 Ghana 1972, 1978, 1979
4 Madagascar 1972
5 Rwanda 1973
6 Ethiopia 1974
7 Niger 1974
8 Chad 1975
9 Nigeria 1975
10 Burundi 1976
11 Congo 1977
12 Seychelles 1977
13 Comoros 1978
14 Mauritania 1978, 1980
15 Equatorial Guinea 1979
16 Burkina Faso 1980
17 Central African Republic 1980
18 Guinea-Bissau 1980
19 Liberia 1980

4 1981–1990 CE

1 Central African Republic 1981
2 Ghana 1981
3 Chad 1982
4 Burkina Faso 1983, 1987
5 Nigeria 1983
6 Guinea 1984
7 Mauritania 1984
8 Sudan 1985, 1989
9 Uganda 1985
10 Lesotho 1986
11 Burundi 1987
12 Tunisia 1987
13 Somalia 1990

5 1991–2000 CE

1 Ethiopia 1991
2 Lesotho 1991, 1993
3 Mali 1991
4 Algeria 1992
5 Chad 1992
6 Sierra Leone 1992, 1997
7 Nigeria 1993
8 Gambia 1994
9 Burundi 1996
10 Niger 1996, 1999
11 Congo, Dem Rep 1997
12 Congo, Republic of 1997
13 Comoros 1999
14 Guinea-Bissau 1999
15 Ivory Coast 1999

Glossary

Afrikaner Afrikaans-speaking, white, South African.

Afrikaans A simplified form of the Dutch language combined with Portuguese and African words.

age regiments Groups of men or women, organized by age, who could be called on for work or warfare.

apartheid Afrikaans word meaning "apartness." Refers to the legal, political and social system that existed in South Africa between 1948–1991.

banning Measure used in apartheid South Africa to prevent someone from attending public gatherings of any kind.

Bantu Large group of related African languages, including Xhosa and Zulu. Literally means "people." Apartheid South African government used "Bantu" to mean a black African. Rarely used today because of apartheid connotations.

Bantustans So-called homelands, created in South Africa, as part of apartheid policy that aimed to set up black self-governing "nations."

barter Using goods rather than money to obtain goods or services.

BCE Before Common Era.

Boers Dutch word meaning farmers; the name Dutch settlers gave to themselves.

CE Common Era.

clan A group of people who claim descent from a common ancestor or ancestors.

colony A country, region or territory occupied or settled by people from another country and usually controlled by that country. The people who settle the colony are called colonists.

color bar Segregation by race or skin color. *See also* SEGREGATION.

constitution The principles on which a state or nation is organized. They may be written down, as in the United States.

constitutional monarchy A constitution that allows for a monarch (king or queen) as titular head of state.

coup A seizure of power, usually illegal. A military coup describes seizure of power by the military.

democracy A system of government in which all adults take part in government, by electing representatives to speak for them.

Difaqane Sotho-Tswana word meaning "scattering." Describes the period of mass migrations and wars in the southeast of southern Africa between 1819–1839, triggered by Zulu expansion. *See also* MFECANE.

drought Continuous absence of rain.

franchise The right to vote.

guerrilla Member of an irregular armed group, and not part of a state's official armed forces.

hominid Member of the primate family *Hominidae*, including humans and their prehistoric ancestors.

homelands Also known as Bantustans. See also Bantustans.

homestead A house or estate and its adjoining land and buildings, especially a farm.

hunter-gatherers People who survive by hunting animals and gathering plants.

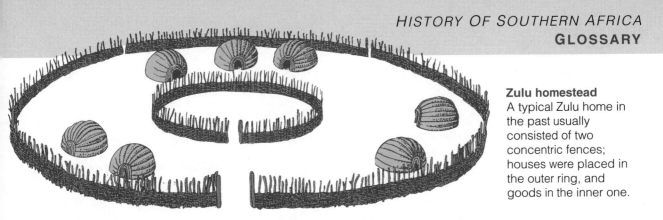

Zulu homestead
A typical Zulu home in the past usually consisted of two concentric fences; houses were placed in the outer ring, and goods in the inner one.

imperialism Either the policy, or the practice, of extending the rule of one state over other, formerly independent, territories.

indigenous Native to a region, belonging naturally to a place.

indentured laborers People who were indentured, or contracted, to work for a certain length of time.

landlocked (country) A country that is surrounded by land (other countries) and has no access to the sea.

Marxist Follower of the Communist principles of the 19th-century German philosopher Karl Marx.

Mfecane Nguni word meaning "crushing." Refers to the period of wars and mass migrations in the early 19th century that followed Zulu expansion. *See also* DIFAQANE.

pastoralists People who keep herds of animals, such as sheep, on pasture land.

plateau An area of fairly high, level ground.

protectorate A state that is controlled or protected by another nation or state. Similar to colony. *See also* COLONY.

racism Belief in the superiority of one racial or ethnic group over another. Discrimination based on that belief is described as racist.

republic A country or state in which power is held by the people, or their elected government, with an elected or non-elected president.

sanctions Economic measures taken by a country or group of countries against another to force change.

segregation Separation, usually of one group of people from another group of people, often on grounds of race, but also gender.

stratified/stratification Arranged or organized in layers. Can describe a social system organized as a hierarchy in which some people are at a higher level than others.

townships Districts in South African towns populated by black South Africans. Soweto, for instance, was a township in Johannesburg.

trekboer The name given to Boers who trekked into the interior of what is now South Africa. The word *trek* in Dutch means to pull.

Veld Open country, grassland. Also spelt *veldt*.

voortrekker Boers who took part in the Great Trek.

Zimbabwes Stone villages or enclosures built by the Shona peoples of what is now Zimbabwe.

© DIAGRAM

Bibliography

Arnold, Guy, *The New South Africa,* New York: St. Martin's Press (2000)

Barnard, A., *Hunters and Herders of Southern Africa: A Comparative Ethnography of the Khoisan Peoples,* Cambridge (UK): Cambridge University Press (1992)

Barthrop, Michael, *The Zulu War,* London: Blandford Press (1980)

Beach, D., *The Shona and their Neighbors,* Cambridge, MA: Blackwell Publishers (1994)

Beinart, William, *Twentieth -Century South Africa,* New York: Oxford University Press (2001)

Brown, M., *A History of Madagascar,* London: Damien Tunnacliffe (1995)

Clammer, David, *The Zulu War,* San Bernadino, CA.: Borgo Press(1989)

Diagram Group, *African History On File,* New York: Facts On File (2003)

Diagram Group, *Encyclopedia of African Nations,* New York: Facts On File (2002)

Diagram Group, *Encyclopedia of African Peoples,* New York: Facts On File (2000)

Diagram Group, *Peoples of Southern Africa,* New York: Facts On File (1997)

Diagram Group, *Religions On File,* New York: Facts On File (1990)

Diagram Group, *Timelines On File, 4 vols.* New York: Facts On File (2000)

February, V., *The Afrikaners of South Africa,* London: Paul Kegan (1991)

Henze, P. B., *The Horn of Africa: from War to Peace,* London: Macmillan (1991)

Kalley, Jacqueline, *Southern African Political History,* London: Macmillan (1991)

Katz, R., *Boiling Energy: Community Healing Among the Kalahari Kung,* Cambridge, MA.: Harvard University Press (1982)

Lemon, Anthony, *Apartheid in Transition,* Boulder, Colo.: Westview (1987)

Nasson, Bill, *The South African War 1899–1902,* New York: Oxford University Press (1999)

Omer–Cooper, J. D., *History of Southern Africa,* Portsmouth, N. H. : Heinemann (1994)

Parsons, Neil, *A New History of Southern Africa,* New York: Holmes and Meier (1983)

Powell, I., *Ndebele: a People and their Art,* London: New Holland (1995)

Robertson, C., and Berger, I., *Women and Class in Africa,* New York: Africana (1995)

Shillington, K., *History of Southern Africa,* Westport, Conn: Greenwood (1999)

Smith, David M., *Apartheid in South Africa,* New York: Cambridge University Press (1990)

Steyn, H. P., *Vanished Lifestyles of the Early Cape Khoi and San,* Pretoria, South Africa: Unibook, (1990)

Thompson, Leonard, *A History of South Africa,* New Haven, Conn. :Yale University Press (1990)

Index

© DIAGRAM

Index

Index